QUEEN MARY'S DOLLS' HOUSE

QUEEN MARY'S DOLLS' HOUSE

Mary Stewart-Wilson

Photographs by David Cripps

EBURY PRESS
LONDON

DEDICATION

To my father Michael Fox, Coldstream Guards,
from whom I first heard of the House.

Title page caption: By permission of Queen Mary, the Cauldon Potteries held certain reproduction rights pertaining to the House. Their official souvenirs were four china models of the Dolls' House between 4½ and 7½ inches high. The most expensive of these was a container with a perforated lid for flowers which cost 12/6 (62½ pence). The model shown here has a lift-off roof, leaving a suitable recepticle for bulbs or treasures.

First published in 1988 by The Bodley Head
Reprinted 1988 (twice), 1989

This edition first published in 1995 by
Ebury Press
Random House, 20 Vauxhall Bridge Road, London SW1V 2SA

Random House Australia Pty Limited
20 Alfred Street, Milsons Point, Sydney, New South Wales 2061, Australia

Random House New Zealand Limited
18 Poland Road, Glenfield, Auckland 10, New Zealand

Random House South Africa (Pty) Limited
PO Box 337, Bergvlei, South Africa

Random House UK Limited Reg. No. 954009

A CIP catalogue record for this book is available from the British Library

ISBN 0 09 182019 7

Text Copyright © Mary Stewart-Wilson 1988
Photographs © The Royal Collection 1988, reproduced by gracious permission of Her Majesty The Queen

Photographs by David Cripps
Design by Trevor Wayman

Printed in Singapore

CONTENTS

Acknowledgements 6

Introduction 9

1 The Building of the House 10

2 The Shell 22

3 The Hall and Games Cupboard 26

4 The Library 33

5 The Kitchen, Scullery, Pantry and Kitchen Service Lobby 45

6 The Dining Room and Strong Room 57

7 The Upper Hall 64

8 The King's Suite 68

9 The Queen's Suite, the Trunk Room and Back Staircase 80

10 The Saloon 95

11 The Mezzanine Floors and Staff Bedrooms 105

12 The Princess Royal's Room 111

13 The Queen's Sitting Room 116

14 The Night Nursery, Nursery Bathroom and Medicine Cabinet 121

15 The Day Nursery and Nursery Lobby 129

16 The Linen Room, Housekeeper's Room and Housemaids' Closet 138

17 The Lifts 148

18 The Cellars 150

19 The Garage 163

20 The Garden 175

21 The House Today 185

Bibliography 191

Acknowledgements

After the death of Queen Mary, the ownership of the House passed to Queen Elizabeth The Queen Mother. It is now the property of Her Majesty The Queen. I am deeply indebted to Her Majesty for her gracious permission to make use of material from the Royal Archives and to have new photographs taken of the Dolls' House which necessitated its closure for one month. I very much hope that these photographs, hitherto unpublished, will provide a fresh insight into the beauty of this unique house and its contents. A proportion of the proceeds of this book will go to charity.

I am especially grateful to the various departments of The Queen's Household for their unceasing help and support during this project. The individuals concerned and their departments are listed below:

The Lord Chamberlain's Office
Lieutenant-Colonel Sir John Johnston
Mr David Rankin-Hunt
Mrs Juliet Marsham

The Master of the Household's Department, Buckingham Palace
Miss Adrienne de Trey White
Miss Heather Colebrook

The Royal Collection Department
Sir Oliver Millar
Sir Geoffrey de Bellaigue
Mr Marcus Bishop
Mr Robert Cook

Royal Library, Windsor Castle
Mr Oliver Everett

The Hon. Mrs Roberts
Miss Bridget Wright

The Royal Archives, Windsor Castle
Miss Elizabeth Cuthbert
Miss Frances Dimond

The Superintendent's Office, Windsor Castle
Major Jim Eastwood
Mr David Whincup

District Works Office, Windsor Castle
Mr Edwin Norton
Mr Michael Thresher

I am extremely grateful to The Hon. Hugh and Mrs Astor; Mr Colin Amery; Mr Anthony Berry and Mr Christopher Berry Green of Berry Bros & Rudd Ltd.; Sir Michael Colman Bt of Reckitt & Colman Ltd.; Mr Hugh Roberts of Christie's; Miss Theresa Buxton of Cartier Ltd.; Mr Warren Davis; Mr Richard Dunhill of Alfred Dunhill Ltd.; Mr Peter Rossiter of the Mail Newspapers PLC; Mr Brian Smith of the Daimler & Lanchester Owners Club; Mr Tony Carroll of the Fine Art Society Ltd.; Mr W. H. Summers of Garrard & Co. Ltd.; Mr Kevin Roberts of Thomas Goode & Co. Ltd.; Mr David Horsden of Hoover PLC; Mr James Hardy of Hardy Bros Ltd.; Mary Lutyens; Sir Simon Hornby of W. H. Smith & Son Ltd.; Lord Montagu of Beaulieu and the National Motor Museum, Beaulieu; The Hon. Richard Beaumont and Mr E. O. Warner of James Purdey & Sons Ltd.; The Royal Warrant Holders Association; Sir Richard Worsley of Pilkington Bros. PLC; Mrs Angus Ashton of the Royal School of Needlework; Mr Kenneth Rose; Mrs Henry Wrong; Miss Rhona Mitchell of Racal-Chubb Ltd.; Mr Richard Haigh of Rolls-Royce PLC; Mr Peter Bucknall; Mr John Sayers of the Gainsborough Silk Weaving Co. Ltd. Their time and knowledge have been invaluable.

I am also indebted to the following for permission to reproduce copyright photographic material: H.M. The Queen, pages 11 and 13; the Hulton Picture Library, pages 17 and 21; and Mary Lutyens, pages 12 and 15.

M.S-W, 1988

Foreword by His Royal Highness Prince Michael of Kent

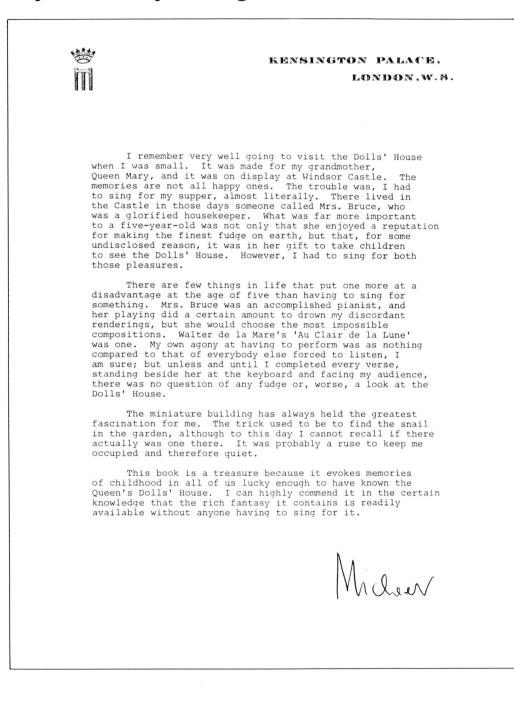

KENSINGTON PALACE,
LONDON, W.8.

I remember very well going to visit the Dolls' House when I was small. It was made for my grandmother, Queen Mary, and it was on display at Windsor Castle. The memories are not all happy ones. The trouble was, I had to sing for my supper, almost literally. There lived in the Castle in those days someone called Mrs. Bruce, who was a glorified housekeeper. What was far more important to a five-year-old was not only that she enjoyed a reputation for making the finest fudge on earth, but that, for some undisclosed reason, it was in her gift to take children to see the Dolls' House. However, I had to sing for both those pleasures.

There are few things in life that put one more at a disadvantage at the age of five than having to sing for something. Mrs. Bruce was an accomplished pianist, and her playing did a certain amount to drown my discordant renderings, but she would choose the most impossible compositions. Walter de la Mare's 'Au Clair de la Lune' was one. My own agony at having to perform was as nothing compared to that of everybody else forced to listen, I am sure; but unless and until I completed every verse, standing beside her at the keyboard and facing my audience, there was no question of any fudge or, worse, a look at the Dolls' House.

The miniature building has always held the greatest fascination for me. The trick used to be to find the snail in the garden, although to this day I cannot recall if there actually was one there. It was probably a ruse to keep me occupied and therefore quiet.

This book is a treasure because it evokes memories of childhood in all of us lucky enough to have known the Queen's Dolls' House. I can highly commend it in the certain knowledge that the rich fantasy it contains is readily available without anyone having to sing for it.

Michael

Introduction

"For a man's house is his castle."
Sir Edward Coke, 1552–1634

For the tourist who visits Windsor Castle today, Queen Mary's Dolls' House is an essential part of his day out. Well over half a million visitors a year pass through the sixteenth-century gateway built by Henry VIII and find their way on to the North Terrace of the castle. Here they can buy a ticket which entitles them to see, from the midst of a continual press of fellow tourists, a short glimpse of this most tantalizing of royal treasures.

Properly constructed miniature replicas of houses were popular from the sixteenth century onwards. Often they might be a family's own house, filled with copies of possessions and used as a way of recording wealth and privilege. Many of these can still be found in private ownership. Handed down through the years, they are not as battered as might be expected. Children of royal or rich families were encouraged to look at the houses from an instructional point of view, "Don't touch" being very much the order of the day!

Unique in the miniature world, Queen Mary's Dolls' House stands where it was designed to be placed, at Windsor Castle. Built for a reigning queen, it preserves for future generations not only information which is rarely found in history books, but outstanding examples of craftsmanship as well. It is also an untouched monument to the genius of its architect, Sir Edwin Lutyens.

Miniature representation has long been universally accepted. The words "doll" or "toy" rekindle a childhood vision of favour or request. But for most of us, miniatures evoke more than our childhood, they are a constant reminder of an elusive ideal. With this perfectly proportioned scale model before them, present and future generations can enter a past age when they visit Queen Mary's Dolls' House.

1   The Building of the House

"It must be useful. It must work dependably.
It must be beautiful. It must last.
It must be the best of its kind."
Alfred Dunhill's maxim, 1907

The idea of a specially designed dolls' house for Queen Mary, the wife of King George V, was first conceived in the spring of 1921 by a first cousin of the King, Princess Marie Louise. Born in 1872, the Princess was the youngest daughter of Queen Victoria's fifth child, the Princess Helena and her husband Prince Christian of Schleswig-Holstein. Although at the age of not quite two, her maternal grandmother described her as "Poor little Louise very ugly", photographs show that she was not an unattractive woman. However, her private life was not a happy one and her early marriage ended in annulment. Her chief satisfaction was to come from the friends she later made from the worlds of music, art and literature.

The Princess was a childhood friend of the Queen and a firm favourite with King George V. Her family's home was Cumberland Lodge in Windsor Great Park, and it was here, after visiting the King and Queen at Windsor during the Easter of 1921, that she watched her mother and sister assembling a collection of miniature furniture for the Queen.

By the 1920s Queen Mary's mania for collecting had become well known throughout her family and the British Empire. Her methods of acquisition ranged from chance discoveries and bargain purchases in shops to point-blank admiration of other people's possessions, which found some owners parting with their treasures as gifts, while others hid their bibelots when it was known that a visit from the Queen was imminent. She was an enthusiastic if somewhat undiscerning collector of antiques, but it was a genuine love of "tiny craft" that filled endless rooms and corridors with specially lit glass cabinets of miniature objects.

All this went through Princess Marie Louise's mind, and on impulse she suggested to her family that she should ask her great friend, the architect Sir Edwin Lutyens, to design a dolls' house for the Queen's personal pleasure. At the private view of that year's Royal Academy Summer Exhibition she met the architect and put the proposition to him.

Between 1912 and 1928 Lutyens was responsible for redesigning eighty square miles of offices, avenues and palaces in New Delhi to house the British Government in India, an undertaking that kept him out of England for the best part of every winter. In spite of these absences and the decline of country house building during the First World War, the Twenties saw a steady stream of commissioned work from the Lutyens drawing board. It was, however, his permanent design of the deceptively simple 1920 Whitehall Cenotaph (originally erected in wood and plaster as a saluting point for the Victory March Past of Allied troops in July 1919) that put him in the eye of the general public and for the first time turned Lutyens into a household name.

From his earliest childhood, when to draw meant to think "and draw a line round my think", Edwin Landseer Lutyens (1869–1944) had had a phenomenal memory for detail. He was the tenth child of the retired army captain and professional horse artist Charles Lutyens, and his beautiful Irish wife Mary. Of an inquiring mind, he also, according to his youngest daughter, Mary Lutyens, combined a natural gift for mathematics with "a creative imagination of genius".

The architect's marriage to the eccentric Lady Emily Lytton might have been a basis for social success, but, in fact, she was too shy to help his career. Lutyens's underlying sense of inferiority, the result of an impoverished childhood and lack of public school education, was in part responsible for a life beset with financial and marital despondency.

Her Majesty Queen Mary.

Sir Edwin Lutyens in the 1920s in a "Napoleon" armchair, two of which are in the Dolls'
House library. His design for these chairs was a favourite one with the architect and was
inspired by a well-known seated portrait of the Emperor.

Her Highness Princess Marie Louise.

However, his innate charm and style, together with his availability for fashionable luncheon and dinner parties, made him a popular guest in London society in the Twenties.

It says much for the sense of humour of the untidy, bespectacled architect that after the initial shock of the Princess's request, he accepted the relatively minor commission of building a dolls' house for the Queen with enthusiasm, and immediately visited the Princess to discuss the project, bringing with him a mutual friend, Sir Herbert Morgan, President of the Society of Industrial Artists. All three were aware that the King and Queen had, after four years of war, come to represent to their subjects all that was best in the domestic and public virtues, and that there had been current for some time an idea of presenting to them a gift as a mark of national respect, thanks and loyalty. The prospective idea of the dolls' house began to fall into place.

In the aftermath of the First World War, many skilled British craftsmen were out of work. From every aspect theirs was a changing world. The new political atmosphere challenged the self-satisfied pecking order of the social ladder of pre-war years, and made certain that an accepted way of life had changed for ever. But the craftsmen's talents were crippled by unemployment, while high taxation on the former governing classes made it difficult for them to commission buildings or goods of a quality acceptable to Lutyens and his contemporaries.

In an attempt to boost a moral and economic recovery, the government had announced that the renaissance of a country "fit for heroes to live in" was to be put to the test in the spring of 1924. Based on an original pre-war idea of Lord Strathcona, the British Empire Exhibition at Wembley Park in Middlesex was to be the showpiece of the Empire, co-ordinating undeveloped wealth and untapped resources with scientific research in a celebration of human enterprise. Lutyens and his friends, among them Sir Lawrence Weaver, Director Designate of the United Kingdom exhibits at the exhibition, quickly realised that the building of the dolls' house could easily be integrated into this project, and would be an invaluable advertisement to promote the names and products of the top British designers, craftsmen and artists of the time.

The next step was to enquire whether Queen Mary would accept such a gift. Princess Marie Louise went to the Queen and told her about the scheme. Her Majesty "was extremely surprised at first but then her artistic and historical sense was fired and she agreed". The Queen also gave permission for the house to be shown at the forthcoming British Empire Exhibition. It would be displayed in a special gallery in the Palace of Arts and the proceeds from the small fee charged for admission would be added to the fund set up by the Queen for the benefit of her many charitable concerns. The Queen was adamant that the Princess should act as an intermediary between the architect, those involved with the house and herself, so that she could be a party to all their ideas.

After Her Majesty's initial acceptance of the enterprise, Sir Herbert Morgan hosted a large private dinner party at the Savoy to which he, the Princess and Lutyens invited various mutual friends, authors and artists whom they wished to involve. At the dinner the topic of conversation came round to a discussion of how historically interesting it would have been if people living in Saxon or medieval England had produced scale models of houses built in those days. There would have been the ill-lit halls, impractical sanitary arrangements, filthy rush-laid floors and sparsely furnished rooms; and if period duplicates had existed of Elizabethan interiors or classical Queen Anne houses that showed the inadequate lighting, heating and plumbing of the sixteenth, seventeenth and eighteenth centuries, how much easier, the guests agreed, it would be to appreciate the modern refinements which their own contemporaries took so much for granted.

Excitement mounted; in her memoirs Princess Marie Louise quotes Sir Edwin Lutyens as saying, "Let us devise and design for all time something which will enable future generations to see how a king and queen of England lived in the twentieth century, and what authors, artists and craftsmen of note there were during their reign." By this time Lutyens was drawing on every menu card available—not even the napkins and tablecloths escaped—enthusiastically filling them with plans and designs. No detail was to be considered too trivial or unimportant; from the attic to the cellar the house was to be a national treasure, an accurate record for children, adults, and future historians, and a monument in minute perfection of all that was best in British workmanship.

No one was to be called upon to delve too deeply into his pocket, it was agreed. Everything was to be paid for by gifts and private donations. Sir Herbert Morgan took it upon himself to act as chairman of an unofficial committee to help realise the three-year project.

In the weeks following the dinner Lutyens swiftly drew up an elaborate set of plans. The house was a completely original design—neither the interior nor the exterior were copies of any existing royal palace, building or other Lutyens commission. Nor, after the first enthusiastic drawings on the tablecloths of the Savoy, was there any idea of designing a royal house as such. The administrative requirements of a royal household would not have conformed with Lutyens's final conception, which was to show an English gentleman's home between the wars. It became in essence the very house that, had his private life been otherwise, he would have liked to live in himself.

Unhampered by a client's needs, he threw himself into a legitimate extension of his pipe dream: the Dolls' House became his home. Nevertheless, he felt that it was only correct that the recipient of such a gift should also feel at ease there, and indeed it very quickly became the "home" of the Queen as well. By October 1921, Her Majesty's diary records that she "went to see the Dolls' House which Sir Edwin Lutyens and the British artists are giving me and are decorating for me . . . I met there Mr Philpot who will paint the ceiling in my bedroom . . ."

A distinctive feature of the Dolls' House was that almost without exception every item in it was specifically commissioned and an integral part of the whole gift—only a few pieces in the house were found in the antique trade or private collections. Lutyens took command of the operation, filing it in his brain under "vivreations", his personal word for fun. Artefacts were manufactured in the finest of the United Kingdom workshops and factories of the era, and the Twining Model Co. was chosen to assist the manufacturers where necessary.

It is easy to forget that the Lutyens team of craftsmen only had access to traditional methods and materials. There were, for example, none of today's super-speed resins, or epoxy glues. Fish-bone paste and heated animal glue made a long process of bonding work, whilst injection

Lady Emily with her daughter Mary Lutyens aged thirteen.

moulding and plastics did not exist. However, there was available to them an unlimited quantity of quality seasoned wood, excellent metals and fabrics, and sound examples of rare stone, all worked by men whose seven-year apprenticeships made them masters of their craft.

The press quickly picked up rumours of the project and upset Lutyens with garbled and inaccurate descriptions: "Such a bore," he wrote to his wife. By August 1921 he was "inundated by the press and all sorts of undesirables have offered things". Everyone, it seemed, was anxious to contribute, and "Oh, the rubbish that turns up for the Dolls' House."

Once Lutyens had sought out and co-ordinated the ideas of nearly 1,500 tradesmen, artists and authors with the gifts and donations from private sources, the Dolls' House Committee under the chairmanship of Sir Herbert Morgan was delegated to pursue items to furnish the house. Lutyens himself ordered several of them. In a letter of 17 August 1921 to his wife he writes that "I have had the first estimates for dolls' house furniture: 13 State frames—£50, and have sent it to Mrs Marshall Field." This was the "first attempt to land a fish" and he went on to say that he awaited the reply with interest. Omitting to tell his wife, he personally assumed financial responsibility for up to £11,000 and it was not until the house arrived at Wembley in March 1924 that he recovered the £6,300 that he had spent, and finally admitted to Lady Emily that he had been "rather fearful of death before repayment as it would have hit me badly!"

The initial shell of the model was erected in his Delhi office at Apple Tree Yard in London, and Royal Academicians involved in the painting of the various walls and ceilings crossed Piccadilly many times to be presented to Queen Mary or to exchange views and opinions with each other. Lutyens's verdict was law, and nothing escaped his personal praise or criticism. Later, after a door and part of his office wall had been demolished to allow its removal, the house was taken to the drawing room of his house in Mansfield Street, depriving his family of the room's use for nearly two years.

His pigtailed youngest daughter, Mary, found that her quick eye and nimble "old enough to be trusted" fingers were invaluable in the unpacking, placing and appreciation of the tiny articles that arrived almost hourly by carrier. To the thirteen-year-old schoolgirl and her father the house was their own private world and enclosed them in a relationship of unexpected depth.

The Queen kept a sharp eye on the proceedings, and found it a favourite wet-day pastime to visit the Dolls' House. Once she came to Mansfield Street with the King, and stayed over four hours, arranging and playing with everything, much to the chagrin of a lady in waiting who was kept firmly outside the drawing room! In January 1924, when the house was nearing completion, she went twice in four days, first with her son "Georgie", the Duke of Kent, when they spent one and a half hours "going over the beautiful miniature things", as she records in her diary, and later with a friend when she "arranged some of the rooms".

Eleven weeks before the opening of the British Empire Exhibition (where for the first time the King's speech was transmitted by wireless to every part of the country and many parts of the British Empire), the house with every item in place was ready to be presented to both the Queen and the public. Still in the drawing room at Mansfield Street, it was unveiled to an eager press, and the national and provincial newspapers of 8 February

1924 carried the first photographs and ecstatic descriptions of this "perfect house of today in miniature".

Finally in early March the house left the Mansfield Street drawing room ready to be reconstructed in its own Lutyens-designed pavilion in the Palace of Arts at Wembley. Packed into numbered wooden crates, simply stencilled THE QUEEN'S DOLLS' HOUSE, it left dirt and chaos in its wake, ". . . oh, the mess. . . . it's awful, I must put it clean," wrote its creator to his wife, as he surveyed the wreckage of his Adam drawing room, "but it will take a long time!" Nine days later the Queen noted in her diary of 25 March that she had walked "about four miles around the exhibition buildings and so on. Most interesting. . . . . visited the Palace of Arts and the small pavilion where my Dolls' House is to stand . . ."

By April 1924 the head of every firm involved had received from Buckingham Palace a signed letter in Queen Mary's own hand describing the Dolls' House as "the most perfect present that anyone could receive", and an invitation to visit it at the Palace of Arts. On 24 June she wrote her final thank you to the architect, asking him to accept a signed photograph of herself "in remembrance of the trouble you have taken concerning my beautiful Dolls' House". She continued:

I know how much thought and care you have expended on this wonderful work of art which is such a joy to look at, and I, as the proud possessor of this house, can never be sufficiently grateful to you for having given so much of your time in order to give me pleasure. The crowds of visitors to the Dolls' House at Wembley are a proof that the public do appreciate your work. With many many thanks, believe me, yours very sincerely, Mary R

Visited by 1,617,556 people, the house was exhibited during the first year of the Wembley Exhibition between April and November 1924. At the close of the exhibition for that year, it was sent to Windsor Castle. In December 1924 a press release stated that Her Majesty the Queen had graciously given permission for the house to be exhibited at the ninth Ideal Home Exhibition to be held by the *Daily Mail* at Olympia the following March.

In February 1925, packed into 45 cases weighing altogether $4\frac{1}{2}$ tons, it arrived at Olympia in West Kensington. Kept under police guard day and night, it took three days to reassemble the building and its contents. An extra charge of one shilling (5p) was made for permission to view the house, and the £5,500 it made was added to the Queen's charitable fund.

At the close of the exhibition in March the house was returned to Windsor Castle. By July of that year Lutyens had finished adapting a disused china room beneath the Throne Room for its permanent position, and the house was opened again to the public for a charge of sixpence ($2\frac{1}{2}$p) per person, this charge, as always, going into Her Majesty's charitable fund. The Queen accepted the offer made by the directors of the *Daily Mail* of the Pilkington "flat" glass case through which the modern public now view it. Contrary to speculation, the house has not been lent out to a public exhibition since 1925, but remains where it was designed to stand, the only completely untouched Lutyens house in existence, a permanent record of a way of life between the wars.

The architect with King George V and Queen Mary and the Duke and Duchess of York admire the house at the Wembley Exhibition, 2 May 1924. The china souvenirs can be seen displayed in the background.

The house in the making, showing the electric wiring and plumbing system.

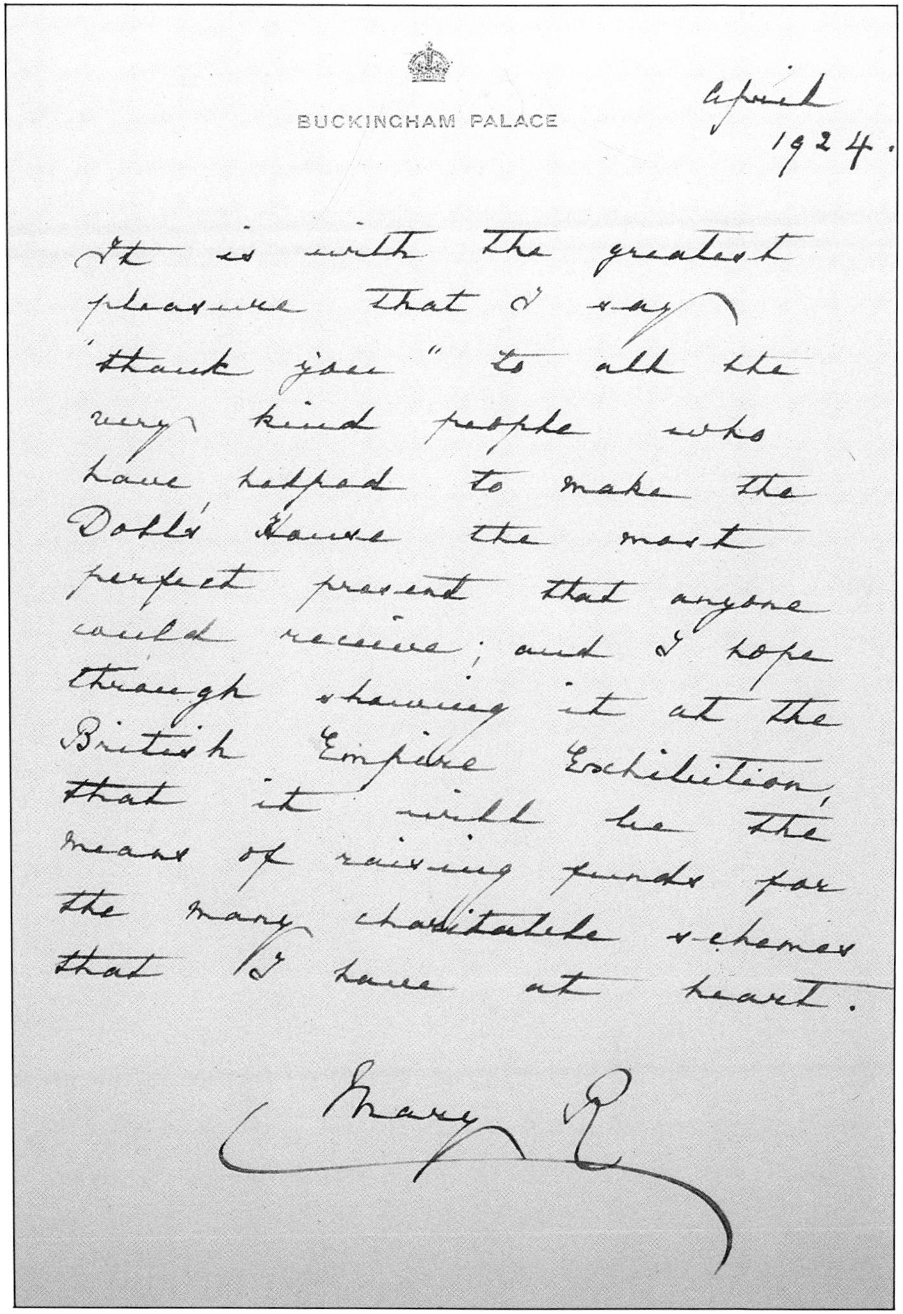

BUCKINGHAM PALACE

April
1924.

It is with the greatest
pleasure that I say
"thank you" to all the
very kind people who
have helped to make the
Doll's House the most
perfect present that anyone
could receive; and I hope
through showing it at the
British Empire Exhibition,
that it will be the
means of raising funds for
the many charitable schemes
that I have at heart.

Mary R

Every firm and manufacturer involved with the house received a copy of this letter from the
Queen. Many of these letters can be found today in family archives.

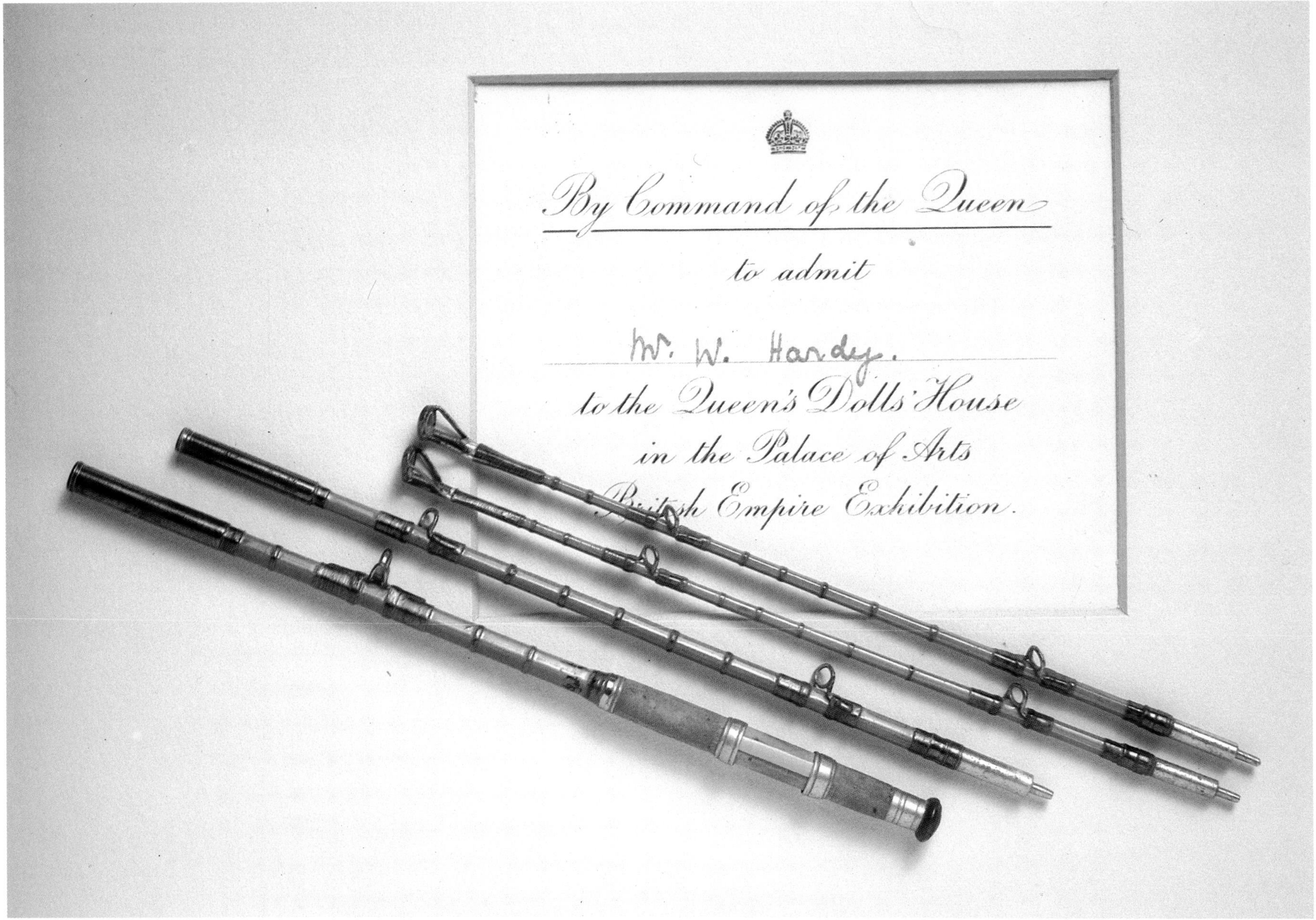

By Command of the Queen

to admit

Mr W. Hardy.

to the Queen's Dolls' House

in the Palace of Arts

British Empire Exhibition.

Miniature of a 16-foot "Palakona" split bamboo salmon fly rod. In three pieces, the length when assembled is 16 inches. It was made for the Dolls' House by Hardy Bros Ltd. and presented by Mr W. Hardy, father of today's Marketing Director, Mr James Hardy, who found this invitation discarded with some rubbish when the factory moved in 1965.

The house being packed up in the Mansfield Street drawing room. Lady Emily found it easiest to ignore this room for two years!

2 The Shell

"The Queen writes she is nervous as to how the Dolls'
House opens and asks questions about the hall door."
Letter from Sir Edwin Lutyens to Lady Emily, 17 August 1921

The Queen's worry as to how the Dolls' House opened was a perfectly reasonable one. The plans showed over forty rooms and vestibules on four elevations, with two staircases, two lifts that stopped at every floor, hot and cold running water in all five bathrooms, water closets that flushed, electric light, a cellar, a garage and a garden.

Lutyens solved the problem with the simple device of a closely-fitting outer shell that could be raised and lowered over the inner fabric of the house from machinery installed in its roof space.

Lutyens had been using classical detail in some form or other since his earliest years as an architect. His chief inspiration came from Christopher Wren, and by the early 1900s this influence in Lutyens's work was paramount: he called it his "Wrenaissance".

The outer shell of the Dolls' House is in classical "Wrenaissance" design with the main facade on the north side. The use of real stone would have made the shell too heavy to move, and so carved and painted wood to represent the creamy white of Lutyens's favourite Portland stone was used.

Built on a scale of 1 to 12, the house is 102 inches long on the main north and south fronts, $58\frac{1}{2}$ inches from east to west at ground floor level and is five feet high at parapet level. It stands on a base 39 inches high measuring 116 inches by 72 inches. On the north and south sides, the base is divided into a sub-base 24 inches high, each side containing 104 interchangeable cedar-wood drawers 11 inches long and $3\frac{1}{2}$ inches wide and deep to store the contents when necessary. The upper 15 inches of the base on the north side hides the machinery for the lifts, the electrical gear, and the tank for the water wastes, a system which no longer functions. On the south side a corresponding basement is hidden by a drawer flap which, when pulled down, reveals the cellar with its groined roof.

The western basement is the garage, hidden in a drawer. The flap lets down and the floor extends, leaving the five car bays under the main building.

Gertrude Jekyll's garden is laid out on the eastern side, in a drawer which extends more fully than the garage.

Every room has a fireplace and the double chimney stack rises through the steeply-pitched hipped roof. This is covered with real slates and opens upwards on the north side to show the storage space for the top of the Otis lift mechanism, and the rest of the now disused water system.

The lead statues of the four patron saints of the British Isles stand on the corners of the roof balustrade. St George and St Andrew face north, while St David and St Patrick, holding the last Irish snake, face south.

With the exception of the ground floor on the north and south sides, which are fitted with French casement doors, the windows are all sliding sashes double hung with lines and weights.

All the facades are richly embellished with swags and classical ornamentation. Immense care has been given to the carving of the flowers and musical instruments, and each mythological face carries a different expression.

The inner shell is constructed in four superimposed horizontal sections. To accommodate the lofty ceilings of some of the main rooms, Lutyens used the traditional architectural solution of inserting extra or mezzanine rooms on all four fronts.

It was an accepted custom for architects of standing to include in their

On the north side of the house the royal coat of arms is set into the classical pediment.

Interchangeable cedar-wood storage drawers on the north and south sides of the base.

plans designs for chimney pieces and fireplaces, as well as the usual fittings, and throughout the house several pieces of furniture that Lutyens had designed either for himself or other clients are also represented.

The Indian Government sent as a gift pieces of twelve different kinds of coloured marble which the architect deployed throughout the house, using their colours as a focus for the interior decoration.

Lawrence Weaver, whose work as an author had contributed much to Lutyens's recognition as an architect, wrote of the Dolls' House in 1924 that "The planning of a strictly symmetrical house like this is one of the shrewdest tasks that can be set an architect." He went on to explain that the rules of the game could easily be encompassed if some rooms were left without windows, and if the facades did not accurately represent the layout of the interior. Apart, though, from one or two short cuts in the domestic offices—hardly surprising when basement space had to be taken up with loaded drawers of garage and garden—Sir Edwin Lutyens, Weaver declared, "has played his most difficult game of planning with serious ingenuity and success".

23

On the south side, over her bedroom window, Queen Mary's coat of arms projects between two Corinthian columns. The supporters are the lion of England on the left and on the right, showing her German paternal ancestry, the stag of Württemberg.

The structure was made by J. Parnell & Son of Rugby. The external and internal painting was executed and donated by the firm of Muntzer & Son, Lutyens's own principal decorators. The oak flagstaff flies the Queen's standard. There is also a King's standard in store in one of the cedar drawers.

3　The Hall and Games
Cupboard

The entrance to the house is through the central glazed doors on the north side, which open into the twenty-inch-wide hall. Lutyens's handling of space was a notable feature of his work, and the main hall of the Dolls' House, rising through three floors with lobbies on either side to give access to the main apartments, is particularly successful in this respect.

The staircase and walls are of white marble, with the addition of lapis lazuli for the geometrical floor pattern. The two lanterns which hang from the zodiac ceiling are the architect's own design, and the method of covering the rod with silk cord and tassel was one that he often used in houses he designed.

The grandfather clock in an oak case is one of seven clocks and two barometers in the house. Mainly designed by Lutyens, these cases and movements are all in working order and were a combined gift to the Queen from the London and Paris workshops of Cartier Ltd.

Passing through the right-hand lobby, glazed doors shut off the passenger lift which serves three floors and a well-equipped games cupboard.

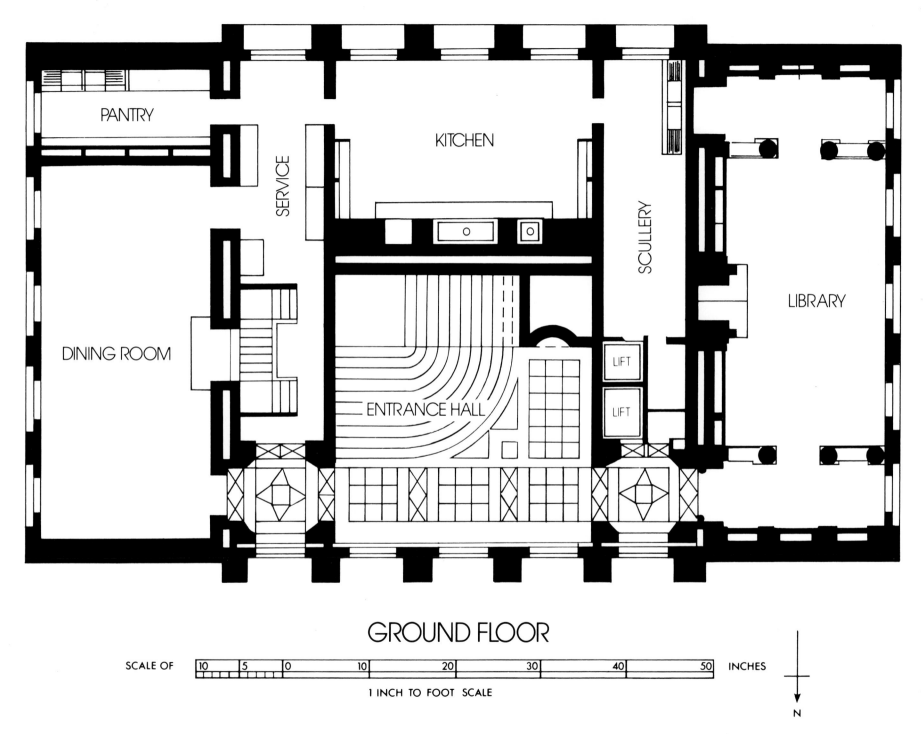

PANTRY

KITCHEN

SERVICE

SCULLERY

LIBRARY

DINING ROOM

LIFT

LIFT

ENTRANCE HALL

GROUND FLOOR

SCALE OF   10   5   0   10   20   30   40   50   INCHES

1 INCH TO FOOT SCALE

N

The games cupboard contains equipment for croquet, cricket, golf and tennis.

Previous pages:
The visitors' book is on the hall table. The large oil painting of Windsor Castle by D. Y. Cameron measures 8 by 5 inches in its gilt frame.

Opposite:
The cricket bat was made by John Wisden & Co. Ltd., and is shown here against a modern standard-size ball.

The golf clubs and bag were made and donated by J. T. Gowdie & Co. The bag is 2½ inches high.

4 The Library

". . . My old, dear and intimate friend Princess
Marie Louise, who is furnishing the Queen's
Dolls' House, asked me some months ago to let
twelve poems of mine be copied small to form
one volume in the library; and I selected the
twelve shortest and simplest and least likely to
fatigue the attention of dolls or the illustrious
House of Hanover."
From the *Collected Letters* of A. E. Housman.
To Grant Richards, 4 May 1923

Reached through the right-hand hall lobby, the library runs the full length of the ground floor on the west front. By the early twentieth century, it was not unusual for the library to be a masculine combination of gun room, study and smoking room, and the Dolls' House library has a cluttered family atmosphere, scattered as it is with periodicals, newspapers, cards and dice.

Panelled from floor to cornice in walnut, it has the lowest ceiling of all the main rooms. The shadowy Roman theme of the painting on the fluted and coffered ceiling was purposely 'aged' by its artist, William Walcot. The furniture and the silver chandeliers were designed by Lutyens.

British rulers have made collections of books down the ages, and the library portraits of the English kings Henry VII (1485–1509), Henry VIII (1509–1547) and Queen Elizabeth I (1558–1603) acknowledge these monarchs' contributions to the sixteenth-century Renaissance of learning in England. King George III (1760–1820) collected what is now the King's Library in the British Library, and Queen Mary herself had a library of nearly five thousand volumes by the end of her life.

There are two unique aspects to the collection of books in the Dolls' House library. The greater part of the literature was commissioned from living authors, being either new work for the purpose (in which case they made a gift of the copyright to the Queen), or their own selection from published work. Their books are in manuscript, often the author's handwriting, and some are illustrated with specially drawn pictures.

The library also carries a quota of printed material. Amongst it, there is a full set of Shakespeare, several bibles and a Koran, a volume of Charles Dickens and all the usual reference books. The manufacture of the books that fill the movable shelves was often fraught with technical problems. St John Hornby, owner of the private Ashenden Press, found his 1½ by 1¼ inch gift of Horace's *Carmina Sapphica* reduced to pulp after an overnight stay in a full-sized binding press.

Princess Marie Louise was the librarian, and she and her friend, the author E. V. Lucas, catalogued and organized the library. A representative rather than a complete library was aimed at and, after selection, the Princess wrote personally to 171 favoured authors of the time. George Bernard Shaw was the only one who did not accept with alacrity the invitation to contribute to the library, and, in the Princess's own words, he refused "in a very rude manner".

Princess Marie Louise also turned her persuasion and charm on no less than 700 artists. She asked them to donate a collection of drawings, watercolours and sketches as well as etchings, lino prints and engravings on metal. These are laid flat, and with scaled plans of the house are stored in the standard way of such collections, in the two large cabinets on the library floor. In fact, the Princess rather overdid this commission for, to keep their pictures flat, most artists pasted their work onto stiff cardboard, thus seriously reducing the space allotted to them in the cabinets. The surplus drawings were therefore catalogued and stored in drawers in the northern basement.

Princess Marie Louise borrowed the King's dispatch boxes and sent them off to be copied. The King was much intrigued to see them in the Dolls' House and enquired who gave her permission. She records that he was somewhat surprised when she announced that she had "just asked for them"!

Above the Chubb safe on the right of the picture, and noticeably empty behind the terrestrial globe, is the gun cupboard. The King was a famous shot, and decided to place the pair of Purdey shot guns from it on a cabinet top (*centre left*) where they could be more easily admired. Too small to fire (they are only 4 inches long), the Dolls' House guns break and load and are typical Purdeys, with two triggers and a top lever. The stocks are finished in wood and fitted with half pistol grips similar to the King's own guns. Purdey's have been gunmakers to the royal family since Queen Victoria's time, and the miniature pair was donated by Athol Purdey, grandson of

the firm's founder, in a traditional leather gun case complete with cleaning rod, tow and oil. The gift also included a shooting stick made to the King's personal pattern, a magazine holding a hundred cartridges and a leather cartridge bag.

The book-binding in the library was the work of seven firms. Most prominent among them was Sangorski & Sutcliff, a firm much used by Lutyens personally, and also responsible for the cyphered design on the leather shelf edging in the library.

William Nicholson's portrait of Queen Elizabeth I, based on the sixteenth-century Armada Portrait by an unknown artist.

The *Royal George*. Built in 1817, she was the royal yacht of King George III.

Briar pipes with the famous white Dunhill spot. Cigars, cigarettes and tobacco were donated by Alfred Dunhill, founder of the firm and grandfather of today's chairman. Matches donated by Bryant & May Ltd.

The Swan fountain pen and inkwell are filled from a large blue bottle of Stephens's ink.

Photographed on a full-sized volume from Queen Mary's collection in the Royal Library at Windsor Castle, this book is the smallest amongst the original contributions, measuring only 1 inch by $\frac{7}{8}$ inches. It approximates to a miniature octavo book, while others in the Dolls' House library are more like reduced folios.

The walnut writing table has nine drawers in front and two cupboards at the back. Cartier made the desk clock *sans mouvement*. It is only $\frac{1}{2}$ inch high. The portrait in the lacquer photograph frame is of the King of the Belgians.

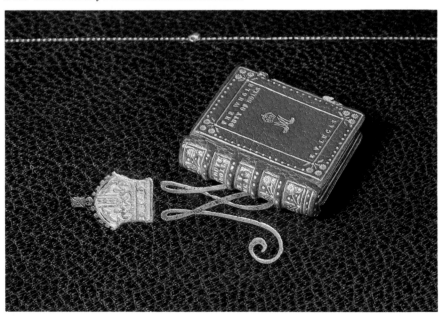

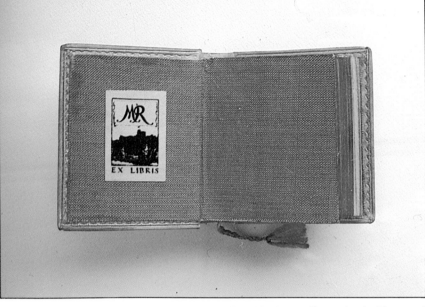

The *ex libris* plate stuck into all the books was designed by Ernest Shepard, who illustrated the Winnie the Pooh books.

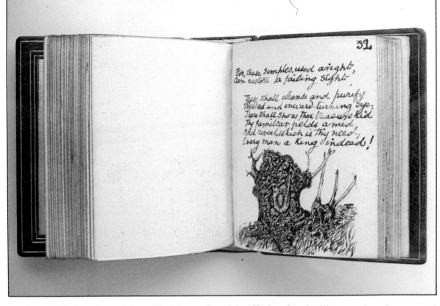

Rudyard Kipling threw himself with zest into his offering for the library, choosing several poems, among them "If" and "The Road through the Woods". He illustrated them with special drawings. The one shown here is from "A Charm".

Sir Arthur Conan Doyle's contribution to the two hundred books on the library shelves was a short story of 500 words in his own handwriting.

King George V was an avid stamp collector and this album donated by Stanley Gibbons contains facsimiles of both English and Colonial stamps.

Dora Webb, A.R.M.S.

THE GROWTH OF WOMAN

H.M. BATEMAN 1922

H. M. Bateman.

Rose Barton, R.W.S.

Three of the 700 drawings stored in the Dolls' House.

Music

Some of the composers whose original work is stored on the Dolls' House library shelves:

BAX, Arnold
BLISS, Arthur
BRIDGE, Frank
DELIUS, Frederick
GOOSSENS, Eugene
HOLST, Gustav
IRELAND, John
SMYTH, Ethel

Drawings and Paintings

Some of the 700 artists whose work is found in the Dolls' House library cabinets and storage drawers:

BIRCH, Lamorna
BIRLEY, Oswald H.
BURNE-JONES, Philip
CLAUSEN, George
DETMOLD, Edward J.
FLINT, Russell
GERTLER, Mark
KNIGHT, Laura
KNOWLES, G. Sheridan
NASH, John
NASH, Paul
NEVINSON, C. R. W.

ORPEN, William
PARTRIDGE, Bernard
RACKHAM, Arthur
RAMSAY, The Lady Patricia (HRH Princess Patricia of Connaught)
ROBINSON, Charles
ROBINSON, W. Heath
ROTHENSTEIN, William
ROYLE, Stanley
SALISBURY, Frank O.
SCOTT, G. Gilbert
SPURRIER, Steven
TAYLOR, Fred
THESIGER, Ernest

Books

Among the books in the library are:

BARRIE, J. M.	*Autobiography*
BEERBOHM, Max	*Meditations of a Refugee*
BELLOC, Hilaire	*Peter and Paul: A Moral Tale*
BENNETT, Arnold	*Christmas Eve and New Year's Eve*
BLACKWOOD, Algernon	"The Vision of the Wind" from *The Education of Uncle Paul*
BLUNDEN, Edmund	*Poems*
BRIDGES, Robert	*Poems*
BUCHAN, John	*The Battle of the Somme*
CHESTERTON, G. K.	*The Battle of Three Horns*
CONRAD, Joseph	"The Nursery of the Craft" from *The Mirror of the Sea*
DE LA MARE, Walter	*Three Poems* and *The Riddle*
DELL, Ethel M.	From *The Knave of Diamonds, Bars of Iron* and *The Hundredth Chance*
DOYLE, Arthur Conan	*How Watson Learned the Trick*
Elizabeth and her German Garden, Author of	*How Mr Elliott Became Engaged to Anna-Felicitas*
"FOUGASSE"	*J. Smith*
GALSWORTHY, John	*Memories*
GOSSE, Edmund	*A French Dolls' House*
GRAVES, Robert	*Poems abridged for Dolls and Princes*
HAGGARD, H. Rider	From *A Farmer's Year*
HARDY, Thomas	*Poems*
HOPE, Anthony	*A Tragedy in Outline*
HOUSMAN, A. E.	From *A Shropshire Lad* and *Last Poems*
HUXLEY, Aldous	*Poems*

JACOBS, W. W. — From *Salthaven*
JAMES, M. R. — *The Haunted Dolls' House*
JEKYLL, Gertrude — *The Garden*
KIPLING, Rudyard — *Verses*
LUCAS, E. V. — *The Whole Duty of Dolls*
MACAULAY, Rose — "The Alien" and "The Thief"
MACKENZIE, Compton — "Richard Gunstone" from *Sinister Street*
MAUGHAM, W. Somerset — *The Princess and the Nightingale*
MEYNELL, Alice — *Poems*
MILNE, A. A. — *Vespers*
NEWBOLT, Sir Henry — *Poems*
NICOLSON, Harold — *The Detail of Biography*
NOYES, Alfred — *Poems*
PENNELL, Joseph — *Thoughts*
QUILLER-COUCH, Arthur — *Verses*
ROSS, Martin (see Somerville)
SACKVILLE-WEST, V. — *A Note of Explanation*
SASSOON, Siegfried — "Everyone Sang"
SOMERVILLE, Edith O. E., and ROSS, Martin — Extracts from the writings of
SQUIRE, J. C. — *Acrostic*
SWINNERTON, Frank — *The Boys*

TYNAN, Katherine — *Poems*
VACHELL, Horace Annesley — *Small Change*
VOYSEY, C. A. F. — *Ideas in Things*
WALPOLE, Hugh — *The House in the Lonely Wood*
YOUNG, Francis Brett — Extracts from the works of, in prose and verse

Reference Books

The Navy   Autographs of eminent officers
The Army   Autographs of eminent officers
Statesmen   Autographs of eminent politicians
The Stage   Autographs of actors and actresses
Stamps   Miniature facsimiles in colour of stamps both English and Colonial in leather case
Stamps   Blank book in blue leather in leather case
Album, 1922   Bound in blue leather. The first left-hand page has the first verse of "God Save the King" (with music) inscribed on it
Who's Who
Whitaker's Almanack
The Post Office Directory
Kelly's Directory
ABC Railway Guide
Bradshaw's Guide

Atlas
Hunting Maps
Motor Maps

Newspapers and Periodicals

The Times
Morning Post
Daily Mail
Punch
Country Life
Architectural Review

Truth
The Field
Saturday Review
Strand Magazine
Pearson's Magazine
The Times of India

Miscellaneous

BERRY, F. L. — The Cellar Book
FETHERSTONHAUGH, Major F. — The Sandringham Stud Book
HILL, Oliver — *The Garden of Adonis* (Illustrated by photographs)
LLOYD, Lady — *A Birthday Book*
MULLER, Frederick — Catalogue of watercolour drawings
SHILTON, Dorothy O. and HOLWORTHY, Richard — *Ancestral Roll*

5 The Kitchen, Scullery, Pantry and Kitchen Service Lobby

"Cookery is become an art, a noble science."
Robert Burton, 1577–1640

The kitchen is the main room on the south side of the ground floor. It is flanked on the right by the scullery and on the left by a service lobby with entrances to both the east side pantry and the dining room. Lutyens's ideal of an orderly life run by efficient, invisible servants is more than realised in this immaculately appointed domain.

Deep cupboards in both the scullery and pantry house the necessary quantities of glass and china, and deep double sinks in both rooms make up for the lack of the modern dishwasher. The size of the taps throughout the house is one of the few exceptions to scale, as an exact one twelfth in the plumbing system would have been too small for water to run through the pipes.

The specially designed plate rack in the scullery can drain the ninety plates of different sizes used for a five-course dinner for eighteen, whilst the slate floor makes for easy cleaning.

Much of the china bears the back-plate of Thomas Goode & Co. Ltd. One of the best known china shops in the world and holder of warrants to no less than nine royal houses before the First World War, the company commissioned and sold glass and china from different factories. Queen Mary was one of the firm's patrons and Goode's undertook to co-ordinate and in many cases donate glass and china throughout the house. As in many large houses of today and yesterday, the names of Minton, Doulton and Wedgwood run through the Dolls' House china cupboards. For the kitchen china, marked with a 'K' to distinguish it from the nursery china marked with an 'N', as well as the storage jars with printed names on the kitchen shelves, Doulton china was used because of its reputation for being hard-wearing.

Although the kitchen is measured in inches and not in feet, there are 2,500 blocks of wood in the floor, and strips of easy-clean slate in front of the coal-fired kitchen range. The two recesses on either side of the two-oven range contain a hot plate and a separate pastry oven.

There is an excellent stock of frying, preserving and baking pans, gold jelly moulds and cake tins, and tinned copper saucepans in five different sizes.

Among the most beautifully turned pieces of furniture in the house are the wheelbacked Windsor kitchen chairs, made from yew. The oak refectory table with a drawer at each end is a copy of the dining room table Lutyens designed for his first married home.

The Chinese lavender jar on the far right of the picture bears out Agnes Jekyll's excellent suggestion in her Dolls' House cookery book, that to "sweeten the atmosphere before guests assemble and after savoury dishes have been prepared", the dried heads of lavender should be placed on a heated shovel and judiciously waved about!

Too small to see in the photograph are three ivory mice in the mouse-trap that was an inevitable part of kitchen equipment of the period.

The kitchen lobby or service area, with entrances to both the pantry and dining room, has two tables (wooden to stop the trays sliding), a hot plate and, like the scullery, a Minimax fire extinguisher.

Copper kettles.

Mechanics at Guy's Hospital in London made the patty pans and some other utensils in gold to "save polishing".

The copper pans are correctly tinned inside.

49

The Twining Model Co. was responsible for making the mincer, the weighing machine and the coffee grinder on the table.

Doulton kitchen and nursery china marked with their respective letters. The mono-grammed key-patterned service for six people was made by the Cauldon Potteries.

The mechanism of the Ewbank carpet sweeper is identical to today's model.

The perfectly equipped scullery, with lead-lined sinks and hot and cold water. A slate floor ensures easy cleaning.

The butler had to go to the housekeeper for articles of scullery, kitchen and downstairs linen. The open door leads into the kitchen.

Commissioned by Thomas Goode & Co. Ltd., Doulton also made and donated the best royal dinner service with a plain gold rim for 18 people, complete with 22 serving and covered vegetable dishes. Two plates from the china cupboards are shown here on a plate from a private dinner service of Queen Elizabeth II.

Opposite:
The butler's pantry, with plenty of room for storing the glass and five best china services. The silver is stored in the strong room.

A bed tray is laid with the Cauldon Potteries breakfast service.

6 The Dining Room and Strong Room

"Very merry, and the best fritters that ever I eat in my Life."
Samuel Pepys, 1633–1703

With a staff entrance from the kitchen service lobby and another from the entrance hall, the dining room faces east, overlooking the garden. The room is at its best looked at as a whole. The carpet, painted to simulate Aubusson, reflects the pattern of the early Palladian ceiling with its merry spirits encircling the earth. It is also an excellent example of how modern and antique design and furnishing would have been blended in such a house.

The copy of the eighteenth-century walnut table in the centre measures $5\frac{1}{4}$ inches when it is closed, and with twentieth-century construction extends to twenty inches. The eighteen "period" walnut arm chairs are three inches high. Lutyens designed the screen made by Cartier Ltd. to hide the carrying of dishes from the service area to the table.

The paintings over the doors are *trompe-l'oeil* and the painted walls carry carved swags of limewood. The pictures are a typical mixture and include portraits of the kings Edward III and James V of Scotland. Under McEvoy's painting after Winterhalter of Queen Victoria and her family (the original hangs at Buckingham Palace), are two small pictures of corners of the Audience Chamber and Van Dyck Room at Windsor Castle,

specially chosen as suitable subjects by Queen Mary and the artist, W. Ranken. Copies donated by Alfred Munnings of three of his pictures are the King's charger "Delhi", a Friesian bull and an equestrian portrait of King Edward VIII as Prince of Wales which later hung in the Paris apartment of the Duke and Duchess of Windsor. The absence of visible picture chains and wires throughout the house is typical of 1920s decoration.

The gold plate and the silver, both in use and on display, would have been fetched by the butler from the strong room on the lower mezzanine floor, reached by the back staircase leading off the service area. Here, apart from the humorous touch of the Crown Jewels, there is adequate space to house the 2,518 pieces of the silver gadroon, thread and shell pattern dinner service for eighteen people. Made by Garrard & Co. Ltd., Crown jewellers since 1843, this, including an eight-piece Abercorn kettle and tea set on a silver tray, was ordered by Lutyens and its cost of £280 was paid in cash by Sir Herbert Morgan.

Also on the shelves is a pair of antique silver candlesticks bored for conversion to electricity.

The still-life oil painting is by W. B. E. Ranken.

The ceiling was painted by Professor Gerald Moira.

Webb's Crystal Glass Co. manufactured the table glass for Thomas Goode & Co. Ltd. This was donated by Mr Minton Goode, grandfather of today's chairman. The place setting is laid with the silver dinner service made by Garrard.

Princess Marie Louise borrowed a linen tablecloth from Buckingham Palace, insured it for £100 and sent it to Belfast to be copied exactly to scale (22 inches). It is one of eight in the Dolls' House, all worked with royal cyphers and the great orders of chivalry.

Price's candles to fill the five candelabra are kept with the dry stores in the cellars.

Behind the steel grille and doors, flawless stones have been used in the regalia. The "ermine" on the crowns is painted in enamel.

7   The Upper Hall

Leaving the ground floor, the marble staircase rises to the two main bedroom suites and the saloon on the first floor. Behind the wrought-iron balustrade designed by Lutyens in the style of Louis XIV, the landing's marble floor is a variation of the geometrical pattern of the one in the hall below.

The architect asked one of his closest friends, the painter William Nicholson, to decorate the classic proportions and deeply coved ceiling of the upper hall. Nicholson complied with an expansive mural of Adam and Eve being forcibly ejected from Eden by a thunderbolt, watched, as he put it, "by their pets"! Painted straight onto the walls, this commission took far more of the artist's time than he had bargained for, and Lutyens had to be firm with his friend to make him finish it.

In the circular niches are busts of Earls Haig and Beatty by the sculptor C. S. Jagger, with Sir William Goscombe John's busts of King Edward VII and Queen Alexandra, on marble plinths, under the side arches to the lobbies.

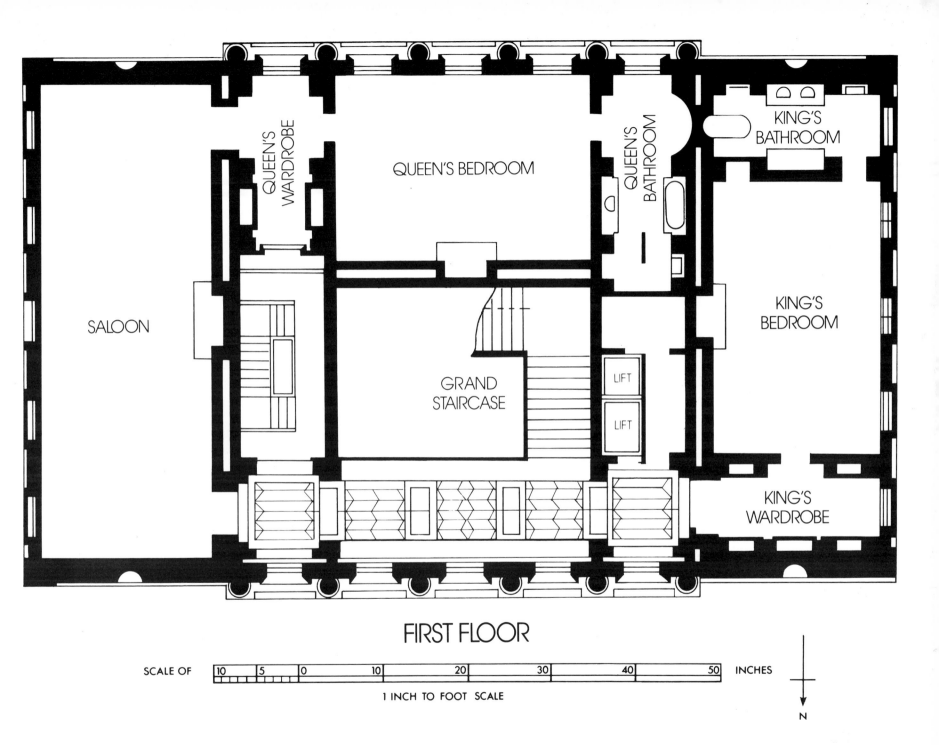

QUEEN'S WARDROBE

QUEEN'S BEDROOM

QUEEN'S BATHROOM

KING'S BATHROOM

SALOON

GRAND STAIRCASE

LIFT

LIFT

KING'S BEDROOM

KING'S WARDROBE

FIRST FLOOR

SCALE OF   10   5   0   10   20   30   40   50   INCHES

1 INCH TO FOOT SCALE

N

Field Marshal Lord Haig (1861–1928). British Commander-in-Chief in France and Flanders during the First World War. Created Earl in 1919.

8　The King's Suite

"Where the quiet-coloured end of evening smiles."
Robert Browning, 1812–1889

From the upper hall, the King's suite of wardrobe, bedroom and bathroom is reached through the right-hand lobby and faces west above the library. To the right, his wardrobe is lined with fitted cupboards on both sides and a field marshal's sword made by Wilkinson Sword Ltd. lies on the lacquer table. On the groined ceiling the artist W. G. de Glehn's scantily-clad maidens are at their *toilette*. The centre light fitting, designed by Lutyens, is made of mother of pearl and ivory and matches a similar one in the private bathroom.

On the bedroom side the wooden carved overdoor in the early Palladian style is the most handsome in the house.

The King's bedroom is dominated by the eighteenth-century state bed. This costly production, with the royal coat of arms embroidered in silk on white damask at the head of the bed, was manufactured and appropriately hung and plumed by the Royal School of Needlework and was donated by the school's founder, Princess Christian, mother of Princess Marie Louise.

Above the chimney piece and marble hearth is Ambrose McEvoy's portrait of the Princess Royal, King George V's daughter. The silver chandelier is a copy of one at Knole, home of the Sackville-West family, and the tapestry fire screen is worked with the traditional vase of flowers on a marble pedestal that was the badge of the weavers of the royal wardrobe in the eighteenth century.

The furniture is of walnut, with comfortable chairs in red damask. Scattered around are favourite books, photographs and one of Dunhill's pipes.

On the left, adjoining the bedroom, marble is a prominent feature of the King's bathroom. Green verdite has been used below the dado rail and for the matching tops of the dressing table and washstand. The handsome verdite bath with six silver taps stands on a marble floor. The dressing table set is made of ivory and there are bottles of hair wash and rose water.

Laurence Irving painted a ceiling of teasing satyrs and zodiac signs, and the pictures are *Punch* cartoons in red lacquer and gilt frames.

The royal coat of arms embroidered in silk on the white damask under the tester of the King's bed. It measures 3⅜ inches in height and width.

George Plank painted the centre of the ceiling with the first lines of the National Anthem.

The dressing-table mirror is made from walnut.
George Plank also painted the wall panels.

Most of the beds in the house are made up with pillows, bolsters,
sheets and blankets.

The thorough attention to detail, seen in the dovetailing of the drawers and the upholstery of the chairs, is evidence of the superb craftsmanship throughout the house.

The carved over-door between the King's bedroom and wardrobe.

The King's wardrobe.

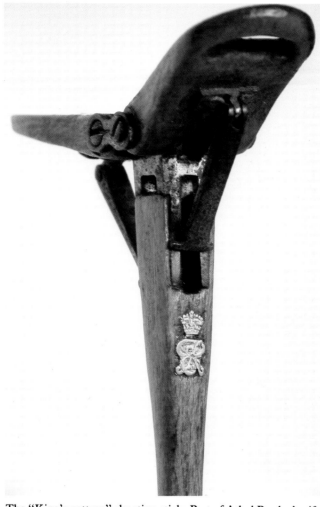

The "King's pattern" shooting stick. Part of Athol Purdey's gift.

Favourite walking and shooting sticks by the connecting bedroom door. Brigg Umbrellas made the walking sticks which are 3 inches high.

The King's bathroom.

The tooth and nail brushes throughout the house were manufactured by the firm of Addis. Their bristles were made from the finest hair available, taken from inside the ear of a goat. The ivory toothbrush is $\frac{3}{4}$ of an inch long.

On one embarrassing occasion Queen Mary caught her earring on the beard of the plumber who was showing her that the lavatory cistern really worked.

9 The Queen's Suite, the Trunk Room and Back Staircase

"For every marriage then is best in tune,
when that the wife is May, the husband June."
Rowland Watkyns, fl. 1662

The Queen's suite fills the second floor on the south side. Her bedroom is above the kitchen, with connecting doors that lead to her bathroom on the right and her wardrobe on the left. Like the King's bedroom, the high ceiling of the main room supports a mezzanine floor on each side above the bathroom and wardrobe.

Both these main suites show the combination of ease and comfort which was beginning to be considered essential to the perfect home of the Twenties. The Queen's bedroom with its walls and bed hung in blue-grey damask is a Twenties pastiche, with furniture that ranges from the Lutyens-designed "Queen Anne" bed, to the modern painted cabinet used as a bedside table with its reading light. The problem of hanging such a stiff fabric as damask on the state beds was overcome by carving the hangings out of wood, and sticking the fabric curtains onto the carved folds. The Queen's bedcover is of blue silk and quilted with seed pearls.

The portrait over the marble and jade chimney piece is of the Queen's mother, the Duchess of Teck, painted by F. O. Salisbury, and the only other picture in the room is a portrait of Mary Queen of Scots by Gerald Kelly.

Two elaborate pieces of furniture are the cream and gilt lacquer cabinet in the style of James II on the right of the fireplace which opens to show five drawers with individual working locks, and the large Victorian wardrobe veneered in amboyna wood, partly fitted with sliding shelves.

Letter-writing and diary-keeping filled an important amount of a lady's time, and a well laid-out desk was a useful piece of bedroom furniture.

Glyn Philpot painted the ceiling which has a centre of perished mirror work.

The carpet was specially woven by the Stratford on Avon School of Weaving and measures $13\frac{3}{4}$ by $16\frac{1}{2}$ inches. Over the doors leading to the bathroom and wardrobe are a matching clock and barometer.

On the right, the bathroom (eight inches wide) is a room of pure fantasy, with shagreen (houndsfish skin) walls supported by columns and arches of ivory. On a floor tiled in mother-of-pearl, the alabaster bath and hand basin designed by the architect have silver taps while, inset behind the bath, the water closet is enclosed in a carved chair.

In the wardrobe, the ceiling painted on wood in oils by Professor R. Anning Bell is a masterpiece of fun, combining the five bodily senses with the four winds and the four seasons.

On the upper mezzanine floor, and close to the staff lift that serves both the back of the Queen's bathroom and the King's wardrobe, a spare room has been turned into a trunk room. The quality of luggage was of great importance, and it was usually made of good leather. As there were always numerous staff and porters available, it did not matter that it was extremely heavy to carry even when empty.

Because of the time it took to travel, clothes had to stay packed for long periods, and the number of changes needed throughout the day and evening necessitated quantities of clothes which were packed in different shaped dressing cases, boot boxes, hat boxes, umbrella cases, trunks and suitcases.

The cypher worked in silk on the canopy behind Queen Mary's bedhead.

The Queen's dressing table set of blue enamel. It includes a pot of cold cream, the only make-up indulged in then by many ladies of the Queen's age. The mirror is framed with real diamonds. The "silk" curtains of the dressing table are painted onto carved wood.

Lutyens designed and Cartier made the clock of gold and blue enamel that stands on the chimney piece.

The best beds had a mattress of horsehair laid on top of a box-sprung mattress, the equivalent of today's interior-sprung mattress. The rubber hot-water bottle was a very modern idea at the time the house was built.

The ceiling of the Queen's bathroom, set in ivory and painted by Maurice Greiffenhagen.

The Queen's bathroom. The floor made from mother of pearl is just 8 inches wide.

Toilet requisites by J. & E. Atkinson Ltd.

The Queen's wardrobe, showing the back staircase.

The seasons and winds painted on the Queen's wardrobe ceiling by Professor R. Anning Bell.

The jewel safe made by Chubb & Sons Lock & Safe Co. Ltd. By permission of the Queen and with the consent of the Cauldon Potteries Ltd., Sir George Hayter Chubb had painted metal replicas of the house made, with a lock and key and a slit in the roof to be used as children's money boxes. The Queen was particularly delighted with these models and asked for two dozen to be sent to Buckingham Palace.

Made by Brigg Umbrellas, with a handle matching one of the Brigg walking sticks in the King's wardrobe.

The banister of the back staircase has the same pattern as the glazing bars of a glass-fronted cabinet Lutyens designed for his own house.

The trunk room. The plain mantelpiece shows that this was an unimportant room. The door on the left leads to a staff bedroom, and the glazed doors to the lift lobby.

10 The Saloon

"Curtsey while you're thinking what to say.
It saves time."
Lewis Carroll, 1832–1898

The saloon, or drawing room, extends the full width of the first floor on the east side above the dining room. Used for formal entertaining, it is the largest room in the house. With no concession to comfort and the two thrones under a silk canopy, the room suggests that in this part of the house at least Lutyens was designing a miniature royal palace. Indeed, by this time he was so immersed in the project that, as his close companion of the time, Lady Sackville, pointed out, he was not paying nearly enough attention to either her, or his work on Britannic House for the Anglo Iranian Oil Co. Ltd!

The six state portraits are charmingly painted. On either side of the thrones the pictures of George III (1760–1820) and Queen Charlotte are by Harrington Mann, copied from the original paintings by Reynolds that now hang in the Royal Academy. At the opposite end Edward VII (1901–1910) and Queen Alexandra by Sir John Lavery are based on the state portraits by Fildes at Buckingham Palace. After some initial doubt, Sir William Orpen, a future president of the Royal Society of Portrait Painters, agreed to adapt his usual free style to paint his first royal portraits, those of the King and Queen. Lady Patricia Ramsay, a cousin of the King, painted the panels over the doors. The specially woven damask material is in the same eighteenth-century style as that in the Queen's bedroom, and hangs between the marble cornice and dado.

The glass vitrines are filled with small ornaments, and the two console tables have elephant-tooth tops.

The music for the piano is a selection from some fifty volumes of published music in the library, the work of twenty-five contemporary composers, which has been photographically reduced to scale.

The door behind the piano leads onto the landing of the upper hall, completing the tour of the first floor.

In the main rooms every fireplace is fully equipped with fireback, dogs and fire irons. These irons are of silver with the Queen's crown and cypher.

The marble chimney piece of the saloon. Above, a portrait of the Electress Sophia of Hanover, mother of George I and ancestress of the House of Windsor, by A. S. Cope.

"The Children of Rumour with her Hundred Tongues", by Charles Sims, on the ceiling.
The dragon that creeps around the bottom left-hand panel warns agile tongues against
unguarded gossip.

The inlaid marble top of the gilt table in the centre of the saloon. This piece of furniture is one of the very few genuine antique pieces in the house, and could well have been an eighteenth-century travelling craftsman's miniature.

The lacquer cabinet has a black and gold exterior and was copied from an existing one at Londonderry House. It measures $4\frac{1}{2}$ inches by $4\frac{1}{2}$ inches in height and width. The gilded stand is $2\frac{1}{2}$ inches high. Presented by the Marchioness of Londonderry.

The copies of eighteenth-century chairs and sofas are not quite 3 inches high. The hand-worked upholstery is in imitation of Aubusson tapestry. The landscapes behind are by Adrian Stokes.

The grand piano was designed by Lutyens and made by John Broadwood & Sons Ltd. The firm is one of the oldest holders of a royal warrant in existence, and was appointed pianoforte manufacturer to King George II. William Orpen's state portrait of Queen Mary is 10 inches high in its frame.

11 The Mezzanine Floors and Staff Bedrooms

Staff rooms on the lower and upper mezzanine floors can only be reached by the back staircase or the service lift.

The supply of domestic staff in Britain had dwindled after the First World War, when former servants found better paid employment for fewer hours' work in offices and factories. Although in many cases modern technology had reduced the necessity for large staffs, households were conscious of the need to accommodate their remaining servants in well-appointed rooms, with better facilities and labour-saving devices.

Distributed on the two mezzanine floors are six servants' rooms, which include the menservants' bathroom with a water closet and the butler's bedroom. The maids' bathroom and water closet is on the top floor by the linen room.

The firm of Waring & Gillow was responsible for contemporary furniture in many large houses, and supplied the Dolls' House with typical, practical pieces for staff bedrooms.

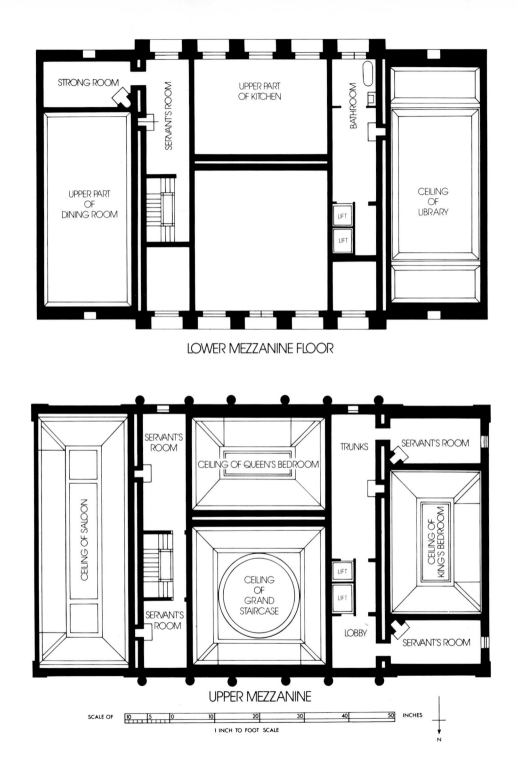

STRONG ROOM

SERVANT'S ROOM

UPPER PART
OF KITCHEN

BATHROOM

UPPER PART
OF
DINING ROOM

CEILING
OF
LIBRARY

LIFT

LIFT

LOWER MEZZANINE FLOOR

SERVANT'S
ROOM

CEILING OF QUEEN'S BEDROOM

TRUNKS

SERVANT'S ROOM

CEILING OF SALOON

CEILING
OF
GRAND
STAIRCASE

CEILING OF KING'S BEDROOM

LIFT

LIFT

SERVANT'S
ROOM

LOBBY

SERVANT'S ROOM

UPPER MEZZANINE

SCALE OF 10 5 0 10 20 30 40 50 INCHES

1 INCH TO FOOT SCALE

N

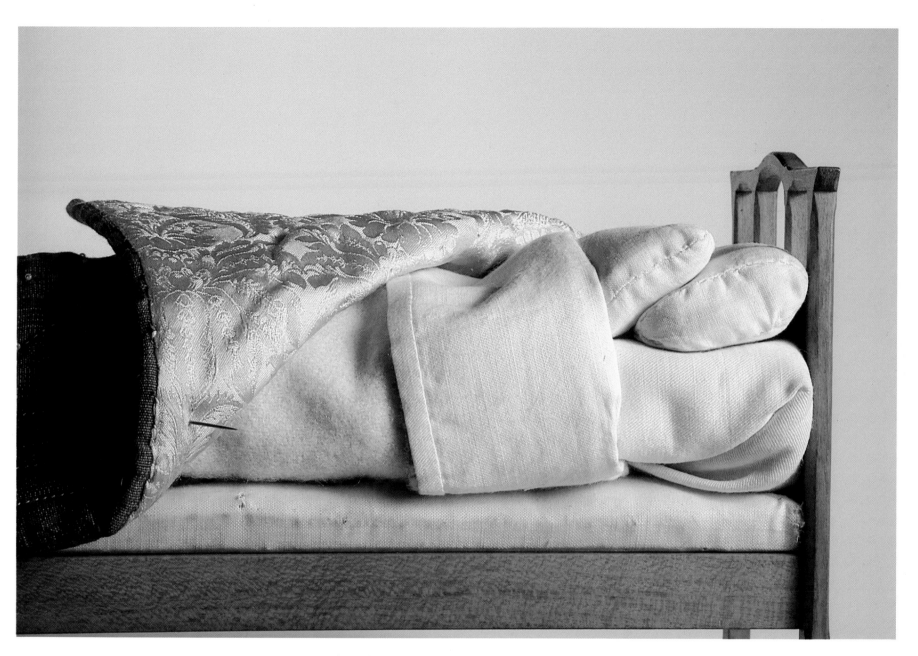

The butler's bed of unstained holly wood. The more important members of the staff had wooden beds and horsehair mattresses.

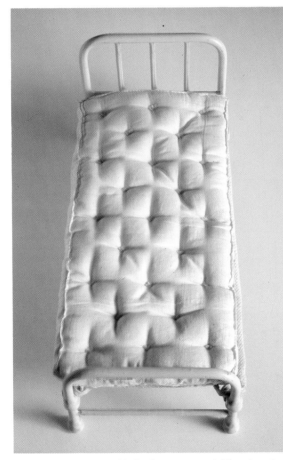

Plain hospital beds with flock mattresses laid on interlaced wire springs were for the junior members of the staff.

A maid's room on the upper mezzanine floor north side.

A maid's dressing table with her sewing basket.

There is a trouser press in every manservant's room.

Washstand in a manservant's room. The picture by Lucy Kemp-Welch is "Bringing up the Guns". The clothes baskets in the bedrooms have attached lids.

The inevitable washstand set of china found in every staff bedroom. This is in the butler's room on the lower mezzanine floor and was made by the Cauldon Potteries, established in 1774.

12 The Princess Royal's Room

"And still she slept an azure-lidded sleep in blanched
linen, smooth, and lavender'd."
John Keats, 1795–1821

The top floor of the house with its two bathrooms, four lobbies and six rooms is the most difficult floor for today's visitor to see clearly. Its many rooms, all ten inches high, are filled with the memorabilia of childhood and family life, and the housekeeper's bed-sitting room and the linen room are also there.

The passenger lift stops outside the north-facing lobby to the Princess Royal's (or the eldest daughter's) bedroom. The room, which looks west over the garage far below, is filled with cream-painted and decorated furniture that matches the hanging cupboard in the lobby.

The bed is a copy of one of a pair that Lutyens designed for his own eldest daughters. Time has disintegrated the pea organically grown to the correct proportion that, true to fairy-tale tradition, he placed under the mattress!

The looking-glass and candlesticks are made of ivory. There are twelve pictures of the "Cries of London" in the room.

The Princess Royal's bed is known as a St Ursula bed. The design was inspired by the Carpaccio picture of "The Dream of St Ursula" in the Accademia, Venice. It is 7 inches high to the top of the frame.

13 The Queen's Sitting Room

"In the midst of this huge model of an Empire
on which the sun never sets,
the centre of public attention is this little house
which the flame of a single candle could gut in five minutes."

From the preface of the original illustrated
catalogue of the Dolls' House at the Empire Exhibition

Placed as it is between the Princess Royal's room and the night nursery, this very personal room contains nothing that is not essential to the character of its occupant. A piece of the Queen's unfinished embroidery lies on one of the chairs. The glass cabinets are filled with a collection of jade and amber; amongst the tiny animals are a water buffalo, a goat and a lion.

Queen Mary enjoyed the oriental decoration and the vogue for cream furniture that were fashionable in the Twenties. Edmund Dulac painted ochre silk walls with golden clouds and water lilies. The rug is a copy of a Chinese carpet of the Chien Lung period and is hand worked with 324 knots to the inch.

The silver Winsor & Newton watercolour paint box on the Queen's desk, photographed alongside a full-size brush.

The glass cabinets are miniature copies of the ones used by Queen Mary.

14 The Night Nursery, Nursery Bathroom and Medicine Cabinet

"Nanny was boss—she was marvellous."
Mary Lutyens to the author

In all households with a nursery, "nanny" was a very important person. Neither staff nor mistress, nevertheless her word was law, and in most cases her responsibility total. The nanny who arrived in the Lutyens's household in 1898, for example, was still with the family when she died 38 years later, and the nanny's rather grand bed in the Dolls' House night nursery can only be interpreted as a mark of the greatest respect. It was usual for the baby of the family to sleep with the nanny, and the Dolls' House night nursery has everything necessary for both of them.

Adjacent to this room, the well-appointed bathroom is for nursery use only. Leaving the bathroom, the immediate lobby on the south side of the top floor is fitted with a pair of walnut wall cabinets. Unglazed and firmly closed against small fingers, these are the medicine cabinets containing invalid food, "Torch" brand hydrogen, Allenbury's vaseline, swabs, bandages and splints. Three padded pneumonia jackets, worn to combat the crisis of this dreaded disease, point to the revolution in treatment brought about since the arrival of penicillin and antibiotics.

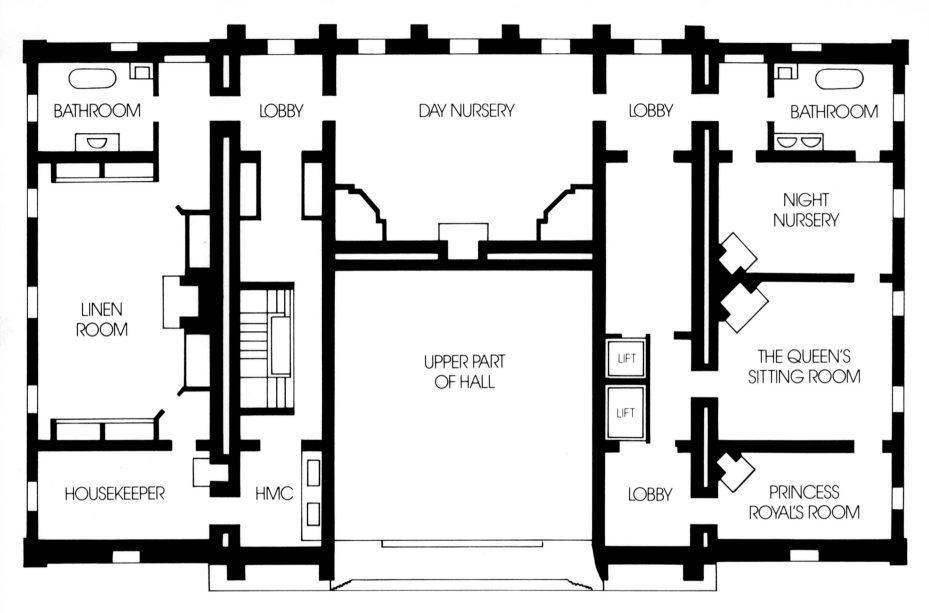

BATHROOM   LOBBY   DAY NURSERY   LOBBY   BATHROOM

LINEN
ROOM

NIGHT
NURSERY

UPPER PART
OF HALL

LIFT

LIFT

THE QUEEN'S
SITTING ROOM

HOUSEKEEPER   HMC

LOBBY

PRINCESS
ROYAL'S ROOM

NURSERY FLOOR

The nursery rooms have everything necessary for the baby of the day. The feeding bottle is one inch long.

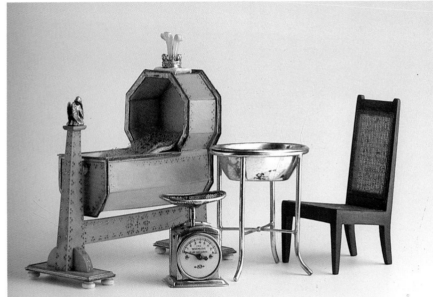

The cradle was especially designed for the house. Made of ivory and applewood with the Prince of Wales's feathers on the hood, it cost £30, and was donated by a Mr F. A. Koenig, a Silesian banker for whom Lutyens was doing some work. The bath is made of silver.

Normally kept in the chest of drawers behind the bed, the lace christening robe and petticoat embroidered with pearls is laid out on nanny's bedcover. The layette also consists of three nightdresses, three vests, three petticoats and two day dresses.

The silver guardian angel at the foot of the cradle.

"Bubbles" by Alfred Heming after Millais.

The nursery bathroom.

One of the three pneumonia jackets in the nursery.

One of a pair of walnut medicine cupboards in the lobby between
the bathroom and day nursery.

15 The Day Nursery and Nursery Lobby

"Where once we dwelt our name is heard no more,
Children not thine have trod my nursery floor:"
William Cowper, 1731–1800

Flanked on each side by useful lobbies that give easy access to both lifts and the back stairs, the day nursery is the largest room on the south front. For the children, everything of interest happened here. Ruled over by nanny, they had their meals (sent up on the special china from the kitchen), played, fought and started early lessons in counting, music and the alphabet. Small children were still very much "seen and not heard", and so were not usually produced downstairs until after nursery tea; then, ultra-clean and uncomfortable visits to the grown-ups took place in rooms which bore no resemblance to their cosy everyday nursery world. The Dolls' House nursery is filled with everything considered essential for this world, and is an excellent reminder of the way in which privileged children grew up between the wars.

Edmund Dulac's illustrations of fairy-tales are painted onto the papered walls, and will keep even today's adults arguing the visible score of either eleven or thirteen stories!

One of the most charming and intricately made toys is the toy theatre. The curtain in it rises on two adjustable scenes from *Peter Pan*—the nursery set with the window wide open and Nanna's kennel, and the underground tree house. That *Peter Pan* was chosen is no coincidence, for James Barrie was a life-long friend of Lutyens, who in turn designed the original night nursery set for the first production of *Peter Pan* in 1904. Lutyens's family were brought up to believe that it was their father who invented Nanna, and that it was from their own night nursery window in Bloomsbury Square that Wendy and the boys flew with Peter Pan to the Neverland.

A comfortable chair for nanny stands by the brass-bound fender that surrounds the hob grate, with the nursery kettle on it for making the baby's feeds. Jars of boiled sweets, rusks, biscuit tins and chocolate boxes are on view. Their contents would have been eaten under strict supervision!

The toy train that draws into Windsor station is four inches long. The fully strung, Broadwood cottage piano has a book of nursery rhymes on it. By the right-hand door is a very early wireless set. The toy cupboards are filled with soft animals, books and amusements, and animals walk two by two into Noah's Ark. Whether or not the parrot is a stuffed or talking model is left to our own imagination.

The glazed corner cupboards in the left-hand lobby hold a pale blue Wedgwood breakfast service, and teatime jams and biscuits.

The toy theatre has two adjustable painted backcloths from the story of Peter Pan.

The hobby horse is 2½ inches long.

A solid, drop-leafed, gate-legged nursery table.

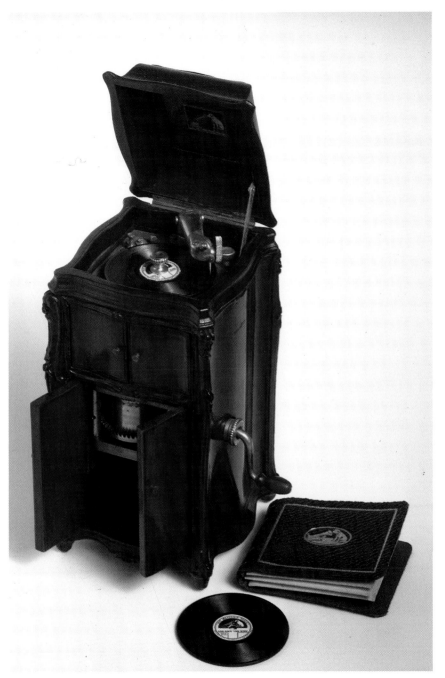

5½ inches high, the gramophone can be fully wound. Seventy people were employed in the various stages of the manufacture of the miniature. The record on it is the National Anthem. Other records include "Rule Britannia" and "Home Sweet Home".

A selection of Pomona toys, considered extremely fashionable in the Twenties.

The breakfast set in the nursery lobby left-hand cupboard was donated by Miss Henrietta Wedgwood. The provisions show familiar names, with biscuits from Huntley & Palmer and McVitie & Price and pots of Tiptree jams.

16 The Linen Room, Housekeeper's Room and Housemaids' Closet

"Quarterly or half-yearly, it is a good plan
for the housekeeper to make an inventory
of everything she has under her care,
and compare this with the lists of a former period."
Mrs Beeton's *Household Management*, 1861

The linen room is the largest in the centre of the east side top floor. To the right is the maids' bathroom, and on the left the housekeeper's bed-sitting room.

Throughout the house there is monogrammed kitchen linen, table-cloths, bathroom towels, sheets, pillowcases and all the usual items required in any house. All this is stored and cared for in the six large unheated cupboards in the linen room.

Although by today's standards the amount seems excessive, linen given to a bride on marriage was meant to last a lifetime. One of the reasons why items well over 150 years old can still be found in many houses today is that to look after linen properly it was "rested" between laundering and use. Frequent washing weakened the fibres, so items taken in strict rotation made it necessary to keep a well-stocked cupboard. There were commercial laundries in the 1920s and the large linen hampers that took two people to carry them to the laundry van show that this was a luxury enjoyed by the inhabitants of the Dolls' House.

The Windsor chairs have the Prince of Wales's feathers on the back, and the picture is by Lady Patricia Ramsay.

The room next door is the housekeeper's own room, furnished with one of the better beds, a comfortable chair and pretty china.

Before leaving the top floor by the back stairs, or one or other of the lifts, it is important to look into the north-facing housemaids' closet. This is an efficiently laid-out room, with its two sinks and teak draining board. Although modern appliances such as the electric Hoover were functional and popular, housemaids were still expected to be downstairs between five and six a.m. to sweep the rooms and fireplaces, and polish grates and furniture.

In the 1920s there was no running water in bedrooms, and copper hot-water cans and jugs were used for filling and placing night and morning in the bedrooms for washing.

6	only	Damask teacloths	1	dozen	Aprons	1	dozen	Turkish bath sheets (large)
6	only	Damask teacloths, square	2	dozen	Glass cloths	$1\frac{1}{2}$	dozen	Turkish towels
8	only	Slips for tables (sides)	12	pairs	Royal sheets (large & small)	1	pair	Turkish bath mats
4	dozen	Table napkins	$1\frac{1}{2}$	dozen	Royal pillow cases	2	only	Cradle mac sheets
1	dozen	D'oyleys, circular & square	$2\frac{1}{2}$	dozen	Royal towels (half huck, half diaper)	4	only	Cradle flannel bath towels
4	only	Diaper teacloths (large)	6	pairs	Cradle sheets	2	only	Baby's bath mats, flannel
12	only	Diaper teacloths (small)	3	only	Cradle pillow cases	6	pairs	Royal blankets (large & small)
10	only	Huck cloths	1	only	Cradle coverlet	4	pairs	Cradle blankets
2	dozen	Plate cloths	4	dozen	Servants' towels, huck	16	pairs	Servants' blankets
1	dozen	Pudding cloths	3	dozen	Kitchen rubbers (knitted)	16	only	Servants' sheets
1	dozen	Roller towels	1	dozen	Knife cloths	16	only	Servants' pillow cases

Previous page:
The linen itself was made in Northern Ireland, the work of an Irish–French lady who
devoted 1,500 hours of her life to the hand-stitching and monogramming of every piece

Linen was tied in different coloured ribbon to denote whether it was for nursery, staff or kitchen.

An electric iron was a modern invention when the house was built.

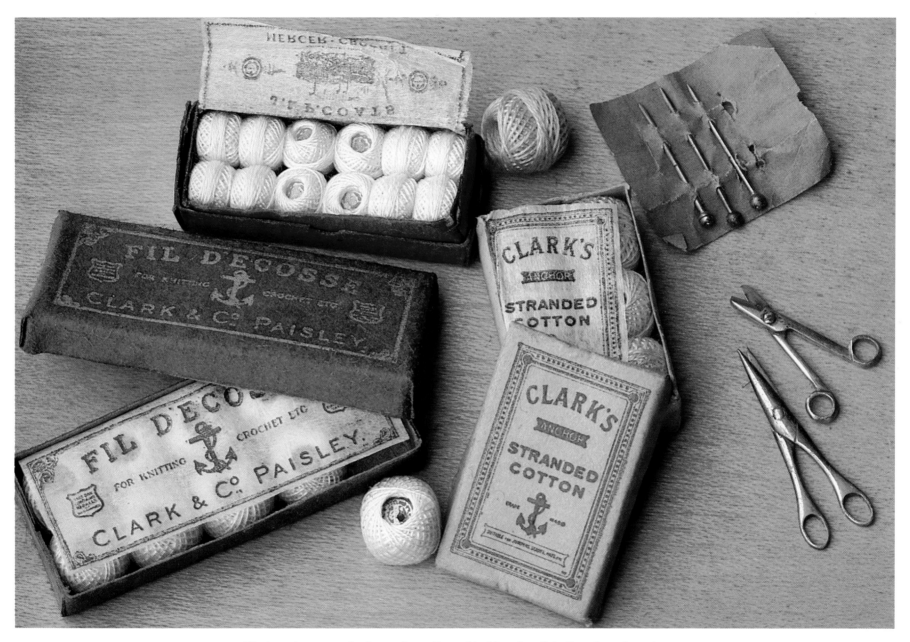

The housekeeper was in charge of mending and looking after all the linen from the various parts of the house.

The treadle sewing machine.

The housekeeper's room.

The housemaids' closet.

Polishing and scouring materials are similar to those in use today.

Dutch tiles were a great favourite of Lutyens, and typical of the era. These are hand-painted and fired replicas of existing patterns.

17 The Lifts

When the house was built, it was the first dolls' house to have both passenger and service lifts. These were specially designed and manufactured by the firm of Waygood Otis Ltd, a company still involved with lift mechanism all over the world today.

Both cars are supported in proper metal slings, and while a safety gear is provided under each, this is not connected up for operation owing to the small size of the model.

The machine for operating the lifts is mounted in a chamber in the roof of the house. The suspension ropes, of which there are four to each car, were made of good fishing line, as this was found to give the best results.

The passenger lift, first entered from the right-hand lobby in the ground floor hall, serves the three main floors, and is controlled by a fully automatic set of push buttons at each floor so that the car can be called or dispatched from any of the main floors.

The goods or service lift is entered from the backstairs area behind the passenger lift and is controlled by a set of three "semi-automatic" push buttons, the third being for stopping the lift at any desired point. The only concession to scale is that for obvious reasons the lift buttons are situated outside the cars!

The passenger car of polished mahogany is 4 inches wide by 5⅝ inches deep and 7 inches high. The floor is alternate strips of oak and walnut.

The service car, made from light polished oak, has no seat and is only 3¾ inches deep.

18   The Cellars

There are five reasons we should drink;
Good wine—a friend—or being dry—
or lest we should be by and by—
or any other reason why.
Henry Aldrich, 1648–1710

Reached by a flight of back stairs, the south-facing basement is a large cellar with a groined roof. This is divided into nine bays. The first half is used for the traditional binning of the wines selected for the house, and the second half for the storage of dry, tinned and bottled goods.

The quality of the wine selected for storage in the Dolls' House cellar was planned with great care and knowledge. The task was undertaken by Francis Berry, then joint senior partner of Berry Bros. & Co. of 3, St James's Street, London, and grandfather of today's managing director of Berry Bros. & Rudd Ltd.

Although Francis Berry's involvement with the cellar came purely from his friendship with Lutyens, this must not be taken as favouritism. Berry's was one of the oldest wine merchants in the business (the company started trading in 1699), and their first royal warrant was given to them by Edward VII, an honour the firm holds to this day. No. 3, St James's Street has been the company premises since it was rebuilt in the early eighteenth century and the name Berry Bros. & Rudd Ltd., as it is now known, was established in 1943.

It is interesting for today's connoisseur to look at the cellar list of the Dolls' House and ruminate on the joys of opening a bottle or two. Anthony Berry, son of Francis, says, "There is nothing that I would not enjoy drinking today."

It should be realised that the amount stocked would only have been expected to last a relatively short time. In the 1920s the owners of large private cellars did not, with the possible exception of vintage port, lay down wine for future consumption as they do now. The lack of inflation between the wars allowed merchants to hold large stocks that were ready for drinking within two years, and weekly deliveries by Berry Bros. to the cellars of the aristocracy and English gentlemen could be up to thirty dozen or more bottles for immediate use. Today's modern tendency to place large orders in anticipation of escalating prices has resulted in the owners of cellarless houses being obliged, more often than not, to store their orders with the wine merchants themselves.

After the wine for the day had been chosen by the master of the house, the butler was responsible for its presentation at table. All red wine and vintage port would have been decanted; port as early as possible on the day it was to be drunk; claret two or three hours before drinking and kept at room temperature without a stopper in order to let it "breathe".

Before the days of stainless steel, large houses used a knife-cleaning machine. Emery powder poured into the machine cleaned the knives, inserted blade down into the sockets. Cleaning the inner brushes of the machine was a time-consuming affair if grease was left on the knives. In the Dolls' House cellar there is such a machine made by Kent.

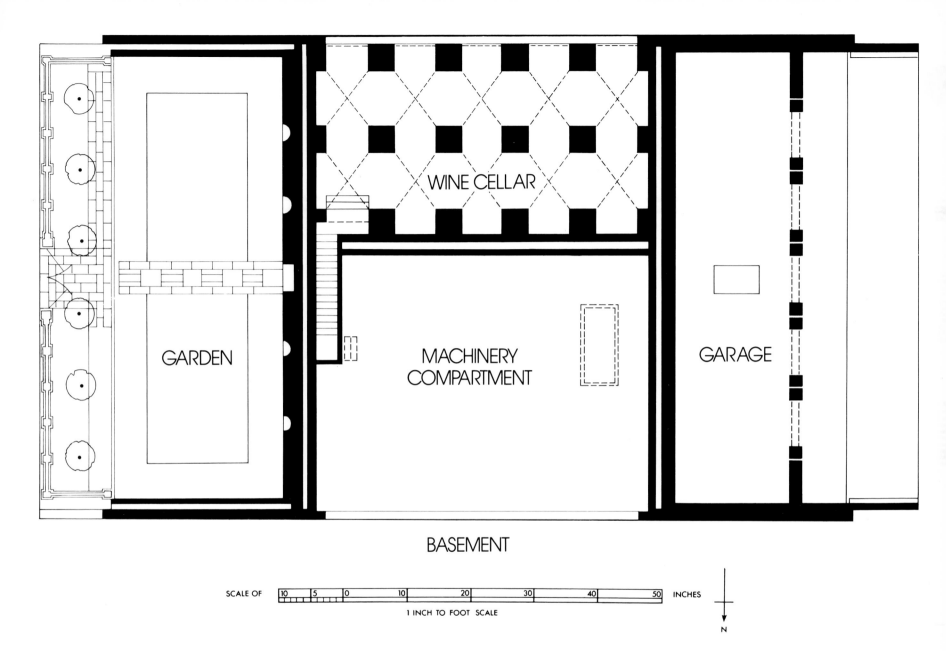

GARDEN

WINE CELLAR

MACHINERY
COMPARTMENT

GARAGE

BASEMENT

SCALE OF 10 5 0 10 20 30 40 50 INCHES

1 INCH TO FOOT SCALE

N

The corks were tight enough to keep the wine in good condition for perhaps forty to fifty years, but it is understandable that after sixty years some evaporation should have taken place.

The ice safe kept in the cellar was a forerunner of today's refrigerator. The tiled side was used for hanging joints of meat. The zinc-lined drawers held lumps of ice delivered weekly by the fishmonger.

The knife cleaner and a selection from the dry stores.

| Name of Wine C.H: Lafite *Claret* Vintage .1875... Bin .41. *C.H: Bottled* |

RECEIVED				CONSUMED				
From	Date	Cost per doz	Quantity	Date	Purpose used	Quantity	Balance	Signature & remarks
Berry	1923	200/-	2 dozen					Use first
					6.			

A careful note of every bottle used was entered by the butler in the cellar book, which was a complete record of the contents of the cellar.

Vintage port in the Twenties had no labels. White splashes of paint on the bottles indicated which way up they should be binned after delivery from the wine merchant.

All the bottles were hand blown to scale by the Whitefriars Glass Co. Authentic printed labels were correctly reproduced by photography and the bottles filled with the corresponding vintages.

Filling the bottles proved to be the most difficult job of all. The wine was introduced into them by means of fine glass pipettes, though the champagne had to be robbed of its sparkle before it could be persuaded to enter!

Not mentioned among the list of stores, but found in cupboards throughout the house, are quantities of Colman's mustard, Lea & Perrins Worcester sauce, Shippham's paste, Jackson's vinegar, as well as toilet soaps from Pears and Atkinson.

Candlesticks were an important part of cellar equipment. Wine was decanted against the flame of a candle, and pouring would be stopped as soon as the wine started to get cloudy or showed the first signs of deposit. Today it is usually decanted against an electric light or white background.

Bass beer was excellent staff refreshment.

Wine Cellar

Dozen	CHAMPAGNE	Vintage
5	Veuve Clicquot	1906
5	Pommery & Greno	1915
5	Louis Roederer	1911
5	G. H. Mumm & Co.	1911
2	G. H. Mumm & Co.	1911 (magnums)
	CLARET	
2	Ch. Lafite, Grand Vin	1875
2	Ch. Haut-Brion	1888
2	Ch. Margaux	1899
2	Ch. Le Prieuré	1918
	PORT	
2	Cockburn Smithes & Co.	1878
2	Taylor Fladgate	1896
2	Warre	1900
2	Fonseca	1908
2	Dow	1912 (magnums)
2	Royal Tawny	
	SHERRY	
2	Amoroso Pale Golden	
2	Oloroso Puro	1872
	MADEIRA	
2	Finest Bual	1820
	WHITE BURGUNDY	
2	Montrachet	1889
2	Graves-Supérieur	
2	Chablis-Moutonne	1904
	SAUTERNES	
2	Ch. Yquem	1874
	BURGUNDY	
2	Romanée	1904
	HOCK	
2	Rudesheimer	
	BRANDY	
2	Grande Fine Champagne	1854
1	Hennessy's ★★★	
	GIN	
2	Dry London Gin	
	RUM	
1	Fine Old Jamaica Rum	
	SCOTCH WHISKY	
¼ cask (28 gallons)	G. & J. G. Smith's Glenlivet, 1910	
	IRISH WHISKY	
¼ cask (28 gallons)	J. Jameson & Sons, Dublin, 1907	

Dozen	FRENCH VERMOUTH
2	Noilly Prat. Litres
	ITALIAN VERMOUTH
2	Martini Rossi
	LIQUEURS
1	Pères Chartreux Yellow. Litres
1	Benedictine, D.O.M.
1	Riga Kummel, Fleur de Cumin
1	Sloe Gin
1	Cherry Brandy
1	Apricot Liqueur
1	Crême de Menthe, Cusenier
	(All above bottled by Berry Bros. & Co.)

APPENDIX

1	Gilbey's Champagne Brandy (in one case)
1	” Whisky (in one case)
2	” Tawny Port (in two cases)
1	” Château Laudenne (in one case)
1	” Vintage Claret
4	Bass Pale Ale (in two two-dozen cases)
8	” Pale Ale
4	” King's Ale (in two two-dozen cases)
1	” King's Ale
2 casks	Bass Pale Ale
2 cases	Gordon and Tanqueray's London Gin
1 dozen cases	Johnnie Walker Whisky

Stores

1	chest tea	2	bottles salad oil
2	packets tea	6	bottles lime juice
2	tins coffee	4	dozen boxes chocolates
1	dozen tins cocoa	2	cases chocolates
4	dozen tins condensed milk	6	tins gums
1	tin Milkal	6	tins toffee
2	dozen jars jam	6	bottles bulls' eyes
18	jars marmalade	6	bottles Maltex
1	packet jelly cream	6	bottles Satines
2	bottles vinegar	6	bottles barley sugar

Dry Stores

6	tins Nugget polish	1	dozen boxes Bromo paper
2	dozen bars yellow soap	3	gross packets matches
6	tins Ronuk	3	boxes club matches
1	box Sunlight soap	3	dozen packets club matches

19 The Garage

"The poetry of motion!
The *real* way to travel!
The *only* way to travel!"
Kenneth Grahame, 1859–1932

When the house was first exhibited at the Wembley Exhibition the six cars in the garage occasioned much comment. Although cheaper cars were just beginning to appear, owning a motor car was still the prerogative of the rich. The Twenties were golden years of motoring design. The horseless carriages of the first decade had made way for vehicles designed as motor cars in their own right.

The great British car manufacturing companies, among them Daimler, Lanchester, Rolls-Royce, Sunbeam and Vauxhall, all of which are represented in the Dolls' House, made their own engines and chassis with a standard body, but it was more usual for the owners of such cars to have special bodywork built to their own requirements by coachbuilders. All the firms invited to donate the custom-built models in the Dolls' House took the opportunity to use the black and maroon colours of the royal livery on their bodywork.

From 1900 until 1943 the official royal motor cars were made by Daimler, a tradition instituted by Edward VII. Today the Queen's official cars are made by Rolls-Royce.

The garage itself is built into a drawer in the western basement. When the drawer is pulled out, it brings the hidden columns supporting the five car bays level with the front base of the house. The front flap of the drawer drops down to a fixed horizontal position to complete an outside yard, stencilled to represent red brick.

A bicycle was a prized possession, and repaid the care spent on it. The brakes of this one are
in perfect working order.

A full-sized Rudge motor-cycle and sidecar cost £95 between 1920 and 1924.

The 1923 40/50 HP Rolls-Royce Silver Ghost seven-seater limousine–landaulet, with tyres donated by the Dunlop Rubber Co. Ltd. and the bodywork painted by F. W. Hooper of Hooper & Co. Ltd. The model weighs 4 lbs whereas the full-scale version weighed 5,200 lbs.

The 14/40 HP five-seater Vauxhall. The radiator badge was made by W.O. Lewis (Badges) Ltd.

The 1922 four-seater 20/60 HP Sunbeam open tourer. This car has brakes on the front wheels as well as the back so that it can be slowed down safely from very high speeds. The weight of the model is 3lbs 14ozs as against the 3,700 lbs of the original.

The replica of the 40 HP 1922–3 Lanchester limousine is 14½ inches long. It was made by the Twining Model Co. with wheels by the Rudge-Whitworth Co. and tyres by the Dunlop Rubber Co. Ltd.

The Daimler limousine motor car with coachwork by Barker & Co. Ltd.

The Daimler station bus made by the Twining Model Co. Ltd.

The King's cypher on the left-hand door of the Vauxhall.

The royal coat of arms on the Daimler station bus.

Queen Mary's cypher on the door of the Daimler limousine.

Silver-topped flasks conveniently placed inside the rear door of the Rolls-Royce.

The Vauxhall wire wheel based on a Rudge-Whitworth patent. Only Rolls-Royce had their own design.

Lanchester built the first petrol-engined car in Britain. Queen Mary's son, the Duke of York (later King George VI), had several in succession for his personal use. The company was taken over by Daimler in the late Twenties.

A Bowser portable tank and pump for pumping petrol either into or out of a car.

The inspection pit and work bench.

The Daimler station bus with a shooting brake body, also used for the staff and luggage. This is the largest car in the garage, and is 18 inches long, 6 inches wide and $7\frac{1}{2}$ inches high.

It was normal for large houses to carry their own petrol pumps and fire appliances.

20 The Garden

"It may safely be said that all good gardening
consists in putting the right plant in the right place."
Gertrude Jekyll, 1922, from her
book in the Queen Mary's Dolls' House library

When Gertrude Jekyll and Edwin Lutyens met in the spring of 1889, she was an eccentric spinster of forty-five, whose myopic eyesight was beginning to restrict her many talents, and in particular her outstanding work in garden design.

Twenty years her junior, the young Lutyens had always nurtured the idea that the garden of a house should complement the whole picture. The meeting of their two minds produced a working partnership of mutual enjoyment: he became her eyes and long-distance vision, whilst she augmented his inspiration with her knowledge of plant and vegetable life.

Their joint commissions reached well over a hundred, and though by the time the Dolls' House was created, Miss Jekyll was nearly eighty and practically blind, being asked to design the garden gave her immense satisfaction, and has left us with an unaltered glimpse of this period of England's gardening history.

The basement drawer which holds the garden with its two-foot trees, rambling roses and a magnificent pair of iron gates is less than eleven inches deep. To have made the garden a permanent fixture would have made access impossible to the interior of the house on the east facade.

The problem of closing the drawer was solved by fixing the trees in front of the gates and balustrade, and placing an invisible hinge the breadth of the garden between the trees and the flower beds. This hinge, when released, allows the front of the drawer to come up, laying the gates, balustrade and trees rigidly horizontal over the hedges and flower beds. The whole drawer can then be pushed into the basement. When the garden is displayed, the drawer is drawn out to its full extent, the front is let down, the trees and gates and balustrade spring into place, and with the other three sides of the drawer forming the garden walls, the complex is complete.

Owing to her failing eyesight, Gertrude Jekyll asked two friends, the Misses Beatrice and Helen Hindley, to make the flowers and trees. It took many hours of structural trials to perfect the authentic shapes and colouring of the flowers in painted metal. Each one is to scale, botanically correct, and made from studies at Kew Gardens. The sisters were also responsible for the bowls of flowers which appear throughout the house. The pots and containers were made from cotton reels.

Beds planted with summer filling of tiger lilies, carnations, sweet peas, poppies, marigolds, gentians and fuchsias. No suitable material came to hand for the box hedges. In the end they were made of specially manufactured rubber and painted by hand.

The trees screw into the base, and their trunks and leaves are made of metal, thickened with specially grown dwarf twigs. Every leaf was shaped by hand.

One of two baby carriages each 3½ inches long.

The garden tools are 5 inches long.

The Atco motor mowing machine with a removable hood is $3\frac{1}{4}$ inches high.

The heavy hand roll-mower is $1\frac{3}{4}$ inches wide.

The grass is made of green velvet.

Two patterns of Lutyens's garden seats made from oak.

The "earth" in the flower pots was roughened with sandpaper and coloured with brown shoe polish. Agapanthus in pots (*far right*) was a Jekyll speciality.

Because the wheels of the lawn mowers are outside the cutting blades, a traditional brick "on edge" is let into the ground between the lawn and box hedge for the wheels to run on.

A bird sits on her eggs.

21   The House Today

"Houses are built to live in and not look on;
therefore let use be preferred
before uniformity except where both may be had."
Francis Bacon, 1561–1626

In the sixty odd years that have passed since it was built, the house, like any other house, has mellowed. Dust has gathered in inaccessible places, walls have faded and paintwork has subtly changed colour.

In 1972, the press was notified and the house closed to the public for two and a half months. All the items in it were removed and given a thorough overhaul by the Restoration Department of the Victoria and Albert Museum. The cars were restored by the Science Museum.

The electrical, mechanical and plumbing systems were renovated. The plumbing and drainage pipes were all intact and in fairly good condition, but the electrical equipment and the lighting circuits were in need of urgent attention. Approximately 1,100 metres of special miniature cable were used to change the wiring in the seventy light fittings from 4 volts DC to 24 volts AC lighting at 2 lumens per square foot. New lighting effects were installed to improve public viewing from outside the glass case, and an operating console was designed to fit into a small room outside the Dolls' House. Each room was wired on a different circuit so that the lights in it could be switched on and off at will.

The crystal chandelier in the Queen's bedroom was electrified with specially devised candle lamps in miniature candleholders. Electric lights were installed in the lifts which were also refitted with modern motors.

The shell raising and lowering mechanism was overhauled and a new electric motor fitted with modern gearing and cable adjusting devices.

And so the house today is ready to face the future, and new generations of young and old will continue to make the special journey from all corners of the earth to see what is justifiably called the most wonderful dolls' house in the world.

Mr E. O. Warner of James Purdey & Sons Ltd. with his original entry in the firm's ledger for the guns in the Dolls' House, 65 years after writing it. Born in 1896, he joined Purdey's in 1918 and has been with them ever since.

Sliding sashes double hung with lines and weights.

Wear and tear on the paintwork of the Queen's bedroom.

The original, unfaded colour of the damask in the saloon is found behind a state portrait. The silk hangings and many of the rugs and carpets in the house were woven by the Gainsborough Silk Weaving Co.

Scratches around the brass door handle and lock bear witness to use over the years. Every lock in the house is in perfect working order.

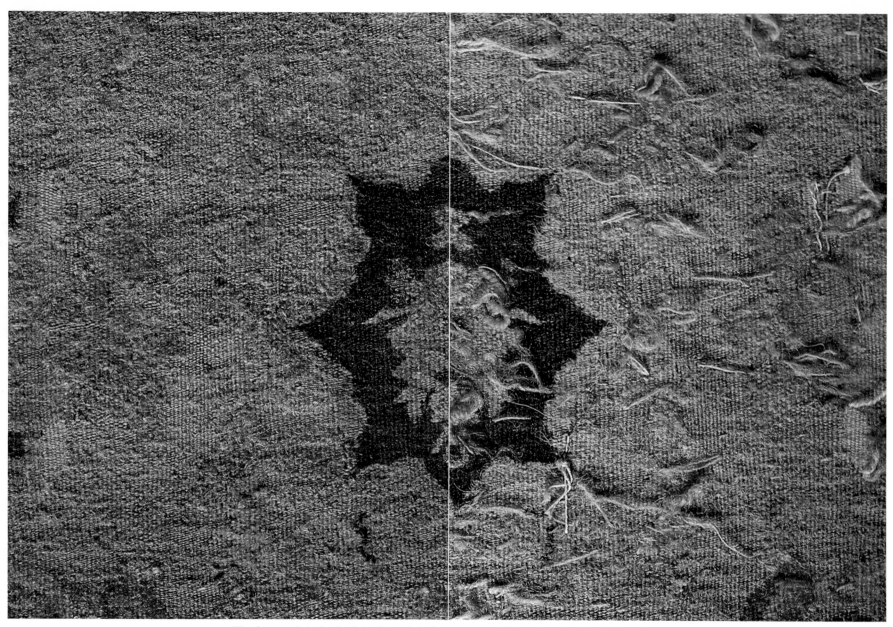

The front and the back of the Queen's bedroom carpet. Woven by crippled children from the Stratford-on-Avon School of Weaving.

Bibliography

Part of the original gift to Queen Mary and one which she in turn presented to many of the donors, were two volumes connected with the Dolls' House, published with the Queen's permission in 1924 by Methuen & Co. Ltd. They were a limited edition of 1,500 copies at a cost of three guineas each.

The first volume was *The Book of the Queen's Dolls' House* edited by A. C. Benson CVO and Sir Lawrence Weaver KBE, the second *The Book of the Queen's Dolls' House Library* edited by E. V. Lucas. Now out of copyright, both these volumes carried an appendix of the names of everyone connected with the project.

In writing my own book I have found the following very helpful:

My Memories of Six Reigns, Her Highness Princess Marie Louise, Evans Bros., 1956.

Edwin Lutyens, by his daughter Mary Lutyens, John Murray, 1950.

The Life of Sir Edwin Lutyens, Christopher Hussey, Country Life, 1950.

Miss Jekyll: Portrait of a Great Gardener, Betty Massingham, Country Life, 1966.

The Private Life of a Country House, 1912–39, Lesley Lewis, David & Charles, 1980.